FRAGMENTS OF LIVES PAST

Fragments of Lives Past:
archaeological objects from Irish road schemes

Edited by Bernice Kelly, Niall Roycroft and Michael Stanley

Archaeology and the National Roads Authority
Monograph Series No. 11

Published by the National Roads Authority 2014
St Martin's House
Waterloo Road
Dublin 4

© National Roads Authority and the authors

All rights reserved. No part of this book may be reprinted or reproduced or utilised in any electronic, mechanical or other means, now known or hereafter invented, including photocopying and recording, or otherwise without either the prior written consent of the publishers or a licence permitting restricted copying in Ireland issued by the Irish Copyright Licensing Agency Ltd, 25 Denzille Lane, Dublin 2.

Front and back cover images
Close-up and full view of an early medieval copper-alloy ladle discovered in Ballynapark townland, Co. Wicklow, on the route of the N11 Rathnew–Arklow road scheme (John Sunderland).

ISBN 978-0-9574380-8-8
ISSN 1649-3540

British Library Cataloguing-in-Publication Data.
A catalogue record for this book is available from the British Library.

Managing editor: Michael Stanley

Copy-editor: Rachel Pierce, Verba Editing House

First published in 2014

Cover design, typesetting and layout: Artwerk Ltd

Printed by Brunswick Press Ltd

Contents

Foreword	vii
Acknowledgements	viii
Note on radiocarbon dates	viii

1. Milk and molecules: secrets from prehistoric pottery   1
   Jessica Smyth & Richard P Evershed
   School of Chemistry, Cardiff University

2. *'Cad a dhéanfaimid feasta gan adhmad?'* Wooden objects from Irish   15
   road schemes
   Caitríona Moore
   Freelance archaeologist

3. The people behind the pots: considering the Early Bronze Age remains   27
   from French Furze, Tully East, Co. Kildare
   Ros Ó Maoldúin
   Ph.D Scholar, School of Geography and Archaeology, National University
   of Ireland, Galway

4. Castlefarm 1 and the working of skeletal materials in early medieval rural   39
   Ireland
   Ian Riddler & Nicola Trzaska-Nartowski
   Freelance Object Specialists

5. An early medieval copper-alloy ladle from Ballynapark, Co. Wicklow   53
   Noel Dunne
   NRA Archaeologist

6. Dress and ornament in early medieval Ireland—exploring the evidence   67
   Maureen Doyle
   Early Medieval Archaeology Project, School of Archaeology, University College
   Dublin

7. Early medieval E ware pottery: an unassuming but enigmatic kitchen ware?   81
   Ian W Doyle
   Head of Conservation, Heritage Council

8. In praise of Leinster Cooking Ware   95
   Clare McCutcheon
   Freelance Medieval Pottery Specialist

9. Witnesses to history: a military assemblage from the 1691 Aughrim   105
    battlefield
    Damian Shiels
    Company Director, Rubicon Heritage Services Ltd

10. Experimental archaeology: making; understanding; story-telling   115
    Aidan O'Sullivan, Mark Powers, John Murphy, Niall Inwood, Bernard Gilhooly,
    Niamh Kelly, Wayne Malone, John Mulrooney, Cian Corrigan, Maeve L'Estrange,
    Antoinette Burke, Maria Kazuro, Conor McDermott, Graeme Warren,
    Brendan O'Neill, Mark Heffernan & Mairead Sweeney
    School of Archaeology, University College Dublin

Appendix 1—Radiocarbon dates from excavated archaeological sites   127
described in these proceedings

References   129

Foreword

If you take the time to peruse monographs 1–10 in this series, you may be surprised to note that there are comparatively few papers that deal exclusively with an individual object or specific artefact type. Hundreds of new archaeological sites have been unearthed prior to road construction during the two decades that the National Roads Authority (NRA) has been in existence, and you will find much information about these discoveries within our seminar proceedings. Most of the papers focus on a site, or sites, with passing reference made to the myriad finds that have been uncovered there. The 2013 seminar—'Fragments of Lives Past: archaeological objects from Irish road schemes'—sought to shift the focus to those items from Ireland's past that offer perhaps the most tangible and enduring connection to the people who created our rich and sometimes troubled history.

The 'Fragments of Lives Past' seminar took place on Thursday, 22 August 2013 at the City Wall Space, Wood Quay Venue, Dublin Civic Offices, and represented the NRA's annual contribution to National Heritage Week. The papers presented on the day explored the theme of archaeological objects and what they tell us about the past peoples of Ireland; going beyond mere measurements to look at the artefacts themselves and to emphasise the human or individual aspects behind the actual objects. What proved to be an extremely successful event culminates with the papers now before you. Among the numerous insights offered herein, you will learn about what Neolithic pottery vessels may actually have contained, the rare survival of wooden objects and the important information they convey, how people in early medieval Ireland expressed identity through their costume and appearance, one of the first locally made pottery wares in Ireland after the aceramic Iron Age and the desperate terror of Jacobite soldiers routed at the Battle of Aughrim, in County Galway.

The NRA had the great pleasure of organising 'Fragments of Lives Past' in partnership with the Centre for Experimental Archaeology and Ancient Technologies of the School of Archaeology, University College Dublin (UCD). Dr Aidan O'Sullivan delivered a paper on experimental archaeology and a number of his students ran hugely enjoyable, hands-on workshops throughout the event, which were the main attraction during the final session of the day. This gave the attendees the opportunity to touch and examine a number of replicas and to talk to the students who made them, using traditional methods and techniques. In addition to expressing our gratitude to all of the speakers for their contribution to the seminar and these proceedings, I would like to pay particular thanks to the UCD scholars who participated in the workshops and helped ensure that the chief goal of the seminar was achieved so successfully.

Fred Barry
Chief Executive
National Roads Authority

Acknowledgements

For their contributions to the seminar and proceedings the NRA would like to express its appreciation to Antoinette Burke, Cian Corrigan, Ian Doyle, Maureen Doyle, Noel Dunne, Richard Evershed, Bernard Gilhooly, Mark Heffernan, Niall Inwood, Mario Kazuro, Niamh Kelly, Maeve L'Estrange, Clare McCutcheon, Conor McDermott, Wayne Malone, Caitríona Moore, John Mulrooney, John Murphy, Ros Ó Maoldúin, Brendan O'Neill, Aidan O'Sullivan, Mark Powers, Ian Riddler, Damian Shiels, Jessica Smyth, Mairead Sweeney, Nicola Trzaska-Nartowski and Graeme Warren. The 2013 seminar was organised by Lillian Butler, Senior Administrator, and Michael Stanley, Archaeologist, NRA. Eoin Scully, NRA, also assisted in the organisation of the seminar. Rónán Swan, Head of Archaeology, and Senior Archaeologists Mary Deevy and Michael MacDonagh, NRA, co-chaired the event.

Bernice Kelly, Assistant Archaeologist, Niall Roycroft, Archaeologist, and Michael Stanley, NRA, prepared the proceedings for publication. The monograph was copy-edited by Rachel Pierce at Verba Editing House and was designed and typeset by Don Harper, Artwerk Ltd, for Brunswick Press Ltd.

Material from Ordnance Survey Ireland is reproduced with the permission of the Government of Ireland and Ordnance Survey Ireland under permit number EN0045206.

Note on radiocarbon dates

All of the radiocarbon dates cited in the following papers are calibrated date ranges equivalent to the probable calendrical age of the sample and are expressed as BC or AD dates, calibrated at the two-sigma (2σ) (98% probability) level of confidence. Appendix 1 provides full details of all previously unpublished radiocarbon dates from NRA-funded investigations described in these proceedings.

1. Milk and molecules: secrets from prehistoric pottery

Jessica Smyth & Richard P Evershed

The Neolithic period is synonymous with a major step in human development: the domestication of plants and animals and the beginning of farming. In Europe, the shift to agriculture starts around 7000 BC, spreading across the continent from roughly east to west over several thousand years. The island of Ireland lies geographically and chronologically at the end of this trajectory, with the first traces of farming activity—in the form of cereals such as wheat and barley, and domesticated animals such as cattle, sheep and goat—appearing around 3800 BC, at approximately the same time as similar practices were being adopted across western Britain, the Isle of Man and Scotland (Whittle et al. 2011, 860–62). These new types of plant and animal are closely linked with new types of site, such as small clusters of timber houses and large enclosures (Illus. 1) (Smyth 2014). They are also closely associated with pottery vessels, which in Ireland, as in many (but not all) parts of Europe, appear for the first time with the arrival of agriculture.

Pottery is a durable and almost ubiquitous archaeological material. It frequently survives, buried in the soil, several millennia after it was deposited and often provides the only lingering trace of past human activity at a particular location in the past. These factors, coupled with the potential for the form and/or decoration of vessels to change over time, mean that pottery is routinely used to date archaeological sites of all periods. The Irish Neolithic is no exception; the pottery vessels made and used by these first farmers have been well documented (e.g. Case 1961; Sheridan 1995) (Illus. 2–5). We know that the earliest examples are round-bottomed and undecorated, with a distinctive shoulder or carination, and that they share affinities with late fifth millennium/early fourth millennium BC pots from northern France and Belgium (e.g. Sheridan 2007, 468–9). Over the fourth millennium BC, decoration appears and vessel forms diversify, with regional pottery types emerging across the island. Many of these changes are closely linked to outside interaction, mostly with communities around the Irish Sea zone. This sharing of traditions culminates in the early third millennium BC (the Late Neolithic) with Irish potters beginning to manufacture a type of flat-bottomed pottery called Grooved Ware, which has its origins on Orkney, in Scotland, in the late fourth millennium BC (Schulting et al. 2010). Needless to remark, the excavation of archaeological sites on NRA road schemes over the past 15 years has greatly increased the number of Neolithic pottery assemblages recorded in Ireland. In the coming years, the next challenge will be to incorporate these new assemblages, along with the many new radiocarbon dates associated with them, into existing typo-chronological frameworks—as, for example, has been already accomplished for Bronze Age funerary urns and food vessels (Brindley 2007).

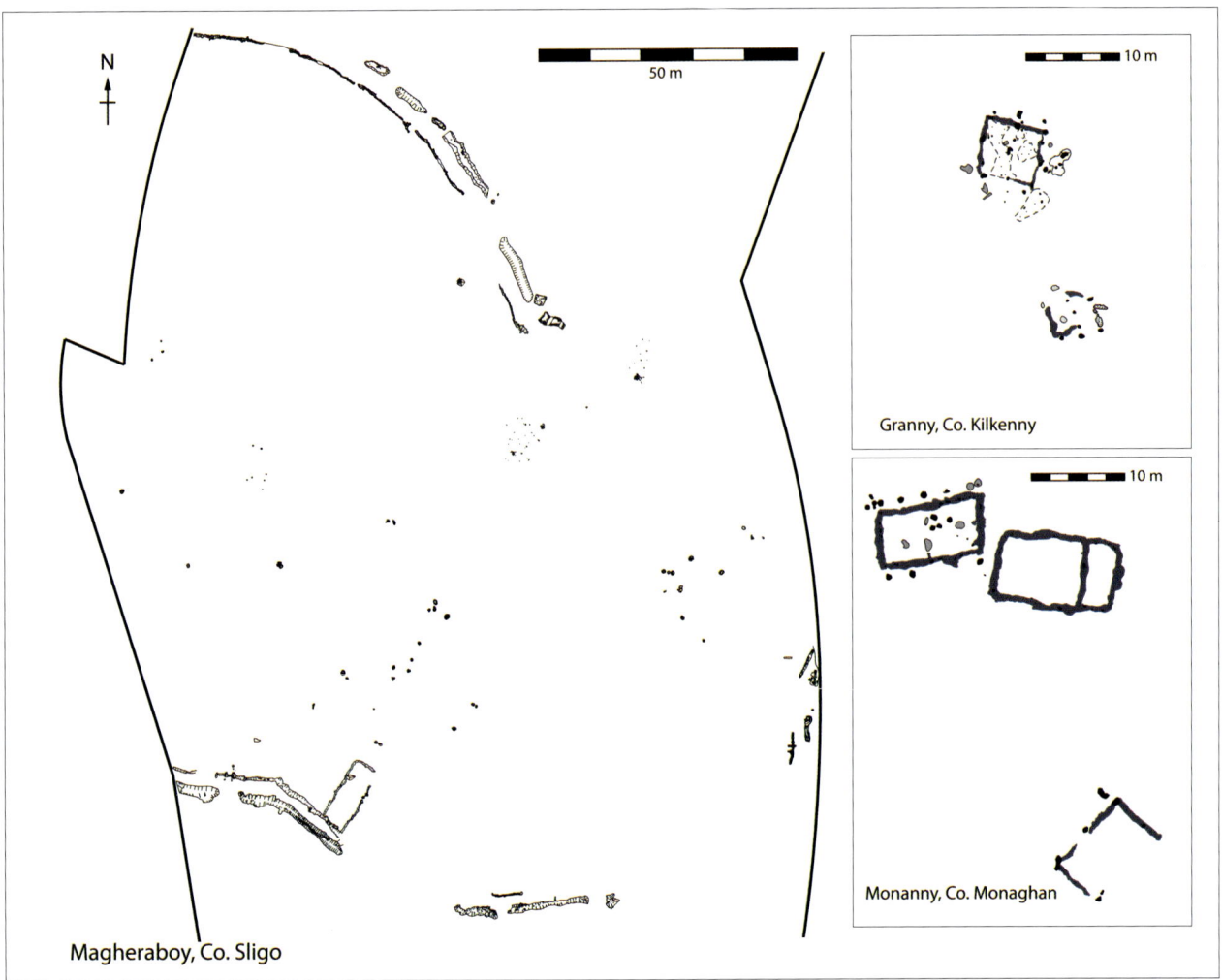

Illus. 1—Plans of an Early Neolithic causewayed enclosure at Magheraboy, Co. Sligo, and Early Neolithic houses at Granny, Co. Kilkenny, and Monanny, Co. Monaghan, which were excavated on national road schemes (redrawn by Jessica Smyth, after Danaher 2007, Hughes 2006 and Walsh 2009).

Pottery and daily life

Pottery is, of course, more than a dating proxy. It is likely that pottery vessels would have been at the centre of domestic life in the Neolithic, part of a wider range of containers made from wood, reeds and other organic materials that were used for storage, cooking and serving, but which only occasionally survive (Raftery 1970; Earwood 1993; O'Sullivan 2001, 78–82; see Moore, Chapter 2). Despite the work that has been carried out on categorisation, distribution and chronology, we know very little about what Neolithic pottery vessels actually contained, which foods were being stored, cooked and served and whether vessels found across domestic, funerary and ceremonial contexts were used in similar ways. Examining the contents of pottery vessels can thus potentially provide great insight into the lifestyles of early farming communities, which was the main aim of the recently completed SCHERD

Milk and molecules: secrets from prehistoric pottery

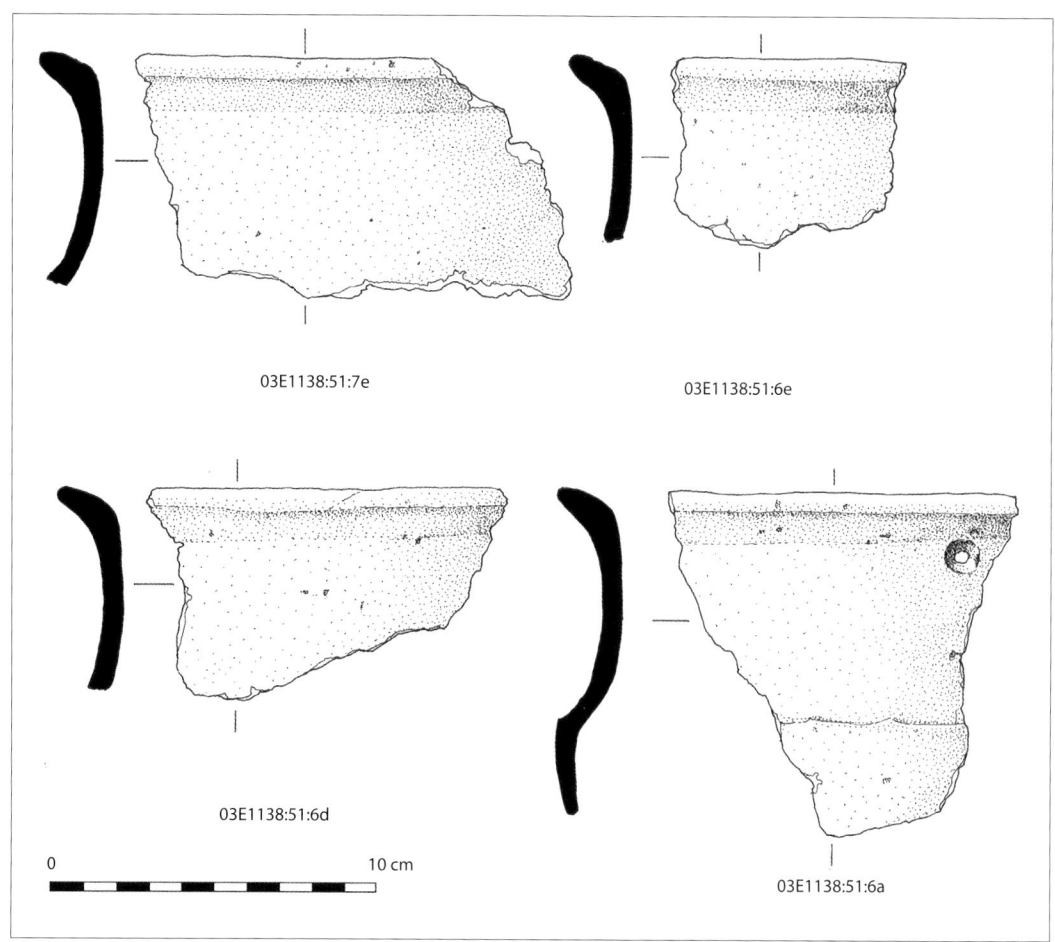

Illus. 2—Sherds from an Early Neolithic modified carinated bowl recovered from domestic rubbish pits at Curraghprevin 3, Co. Cork, on the M8 Rathcormac–Fermoy motorway (Rhoda Cronin-Allanic).

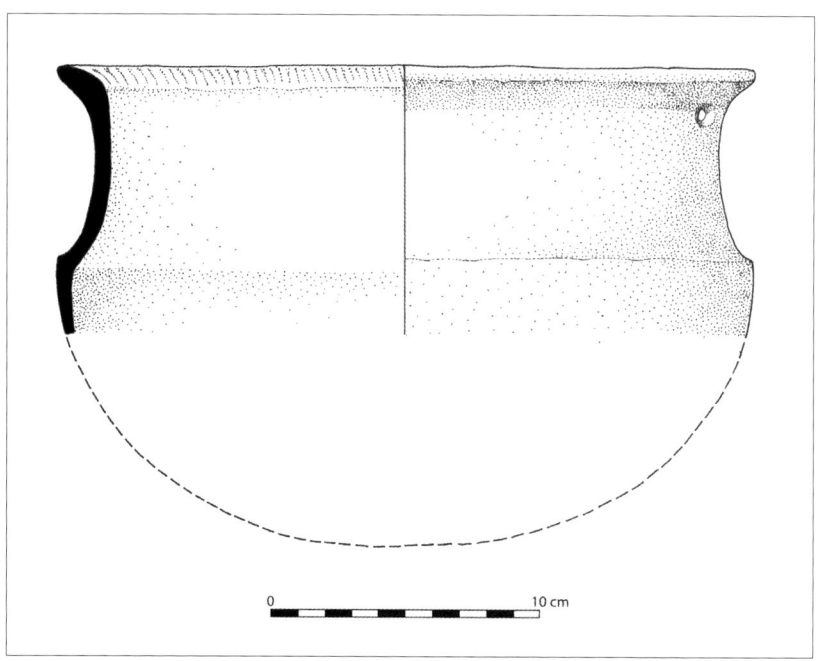

Illus. 3— Reconstruction of the modified carinated bowl from Curraghprevin 3 (Rhoda Cronin-Allanic).

Fragments of Lives Past

Illus. 4—Neolithic pottery (centre) being excavated at Monanny, Co. Monaghan (Irish Archaeological Consultancy Ltd).

Illus. 5—Early/Middle Neolithic pottery from an enclosed Neolithic settlement at Tullahedy, Co. Tipperary, on the M7 Nenagh–Limerick motorway (Department of Archaeology, University College Cork).

project (a Study of Cuisine and animal Husbandry among Early farmers via Residue analysis and radiocarbon Dating). SCHERD was a two-year research project based at the Organic Geochemistry Unit in the School of Chemistry at the University of Bristol. It saw the systematic analysis of organic residues in nearly 500 pots from 15 Irish Neolithic sites.

Organic residues—such as charred food remains, or wax or resin sealants—sometimes adhere to the surfaces of ancient pots. The type of organic residue most commonly encountered and analysed, however, are absorbed residues. In Western Europe at least, prehistoric pottery is unglazed and the porous nature of unglazed vessels means that during the processing of food, lipids such as animal fats, plant oils and plant waxes are absorbed into the vessel wall. In this state, lipids can survive burial for several thousand years and can be successfully extracted from potsherds in the laboratory before being identified and quantified using a suite of modern analytical techniques. Of the 15 Neolithic sites examined as part of the SCHERD project, seven were recently excavated on national road schemes. Below we discuss results from three Early Neolithic sites: a causewayed enclosure at Magheraboy, Co. Sligo, excavated on the N4 Sligo Inner Relief Road; and two house sites, at Kilmainham 1C, Co. Meath, and at Monanny, Co. Monaghan, excavated on the M3 Clonee–North of Kells motorway and the N2 Carrickmacross–Aclint Road Realignment, respectively (Illus. 1 & 6) (Danaher 2007; Walsh 2006; Walsh et al. 2011).[1]

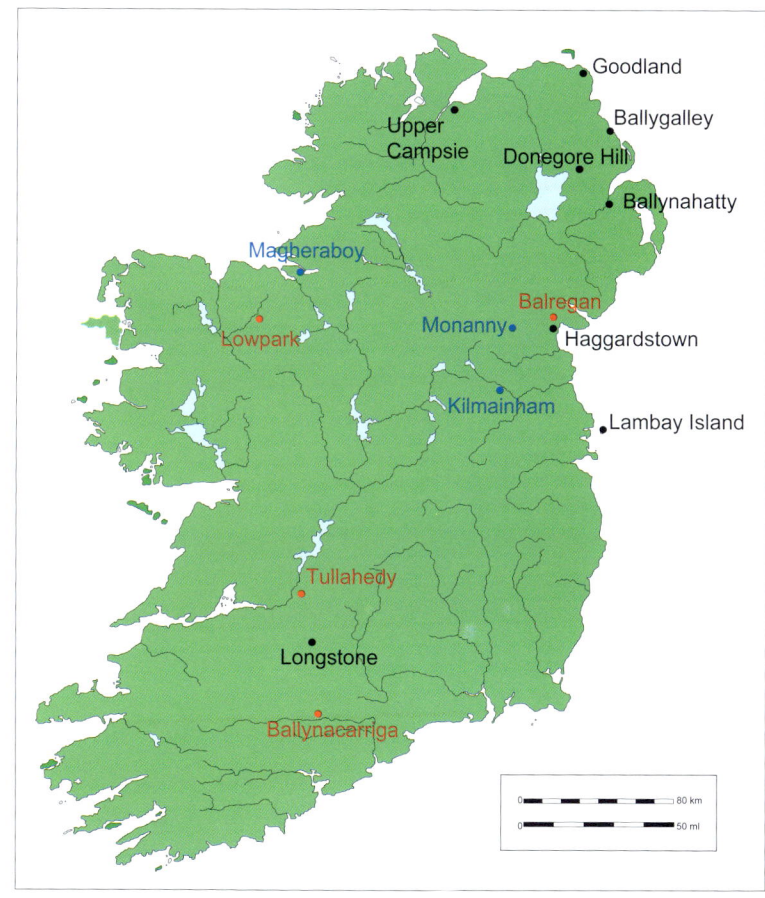

Illus. 6—Location map of SCHERD sites. Sites excavated on national road schemes are marked in red, with the Early Neolithic sites discussed in the text marked in blue (Jessica Smyth).

---

[1] Magheraboy 2C: NGR 168690, 335180; height 47 m OD; Excavation Licence No. 03E0538; Excavation Director Ed Danaher.
Monanny 1: NGR 284280, 305240; height 37 m OD; Excavation Licence No. 03E0888; Excavation Director Fintan Walsh.
Kilmainham 1C: NGR 275700, 274100; height 59–63 m OD; Excavation Reg. No. E3140; Ministerial Direction No. A029; Excavation Director Fintan Walsh.

From site to laboratory

Irish prehistoric pottery is generally very friable and most material emerges from the ground in pieces (potsherds), excavated sometimes from the structural elements of buildings (slot-trenches or post-holes), from the fill of pits or from within occupation surfaces. They can also occur out of context, in the ploughsoil. These potsherds are usually cleaned post-excavation and their location logged, before being handed over to a pottery specialist for identification. Where possible, specialists will attempt to establish the minimum number of vessels from a site or a specific feature and, in addition to assigning sherds to vessels of a certain style, type and relative date, generally note the condition of the material (freshly broken or abraded), the quality of fabric and how vessels were constructed. The assemblage is usually compared and contrasted with assemblages of similar date from across the island, and sometimes beyond, and both exceptional and representative sherds may be illustrated. Most of the pottery analysed for SCHERD was sampled at this stage, post-specialist analysis, as it was helpful to know which vessels were being sampled, where exactly these vessels came from and how they related to the rest of the assemblage.

In terms of the most suitable samples for organic residue analysis, experimental work (see Evershed 2008) has demonstrated that lipids are most abundant in the rim and upper body of vessels. Experience has also shown that while the average lipid concentration in an archaeological potsherd is 100 µg per gram of pottery, concentrations below 5 µg/g cannot be reliably interpreted owing to problems of contamination. On any given site, the percentage of sherds with lipid concentrations greater than 5 µg/g can range from 70–80% to as low as 10%. A 'magic number' of 30 sherds, each representing a different vessel, is thus routinely used as a sampling guide to ensure that a statistically reliable amount of data is obtained. Washing sherds during post-excavation processing can also result in the loss of organic residues, so unwashed sherds are preferred.

To begin with, a small portion (2–3 g) of a sherd from each vessel to be analysed is surface-cleaned, chipped off and ground to a fine powder. Solvents are added to the powder to extract the lipids, and this lipid extract is filtered and purified before being analysed using a gas chromatograph (GC), which separates out the mixture of lipids into its individual components, or compounds, and displays this information as a gas chromatogram. Naturally enough, different pot contents will be represented by different lipid mixtures of varying combinations and quantities of these individual lipid compounds, which in turn produce different-looking gas chromatograms. The successful identification of the commodities processed in pottery vessels rests on comparing the composition of archaeological lipid mixtures with those from modern reference materials, while—crucially—taking into account the changes brought about by degradation during burial and/or vessel use.

For example, by far the most common lipid mixture observed in ancient pots is that originating from animal fats. In fresh animal fats and plant oils, lipid compounds called triacylglycerols (TAGs) are very abundant, but break down over time to diacylglycerols (DAGs), monoacylglycerols (MAGs) and free fatty acids. This has been verified through simulated degradation experiments in the laboratory, with gas chromatograms of fresh and degraded animal fats looking quite different (Illus. 7). Knowing that these chemical changes occur allows us to work backwards to reconstruct the original commodity. Lipid residues in the Irish Neolithic pots analysed as part of SCHERD were dominated by degraded animal fats.

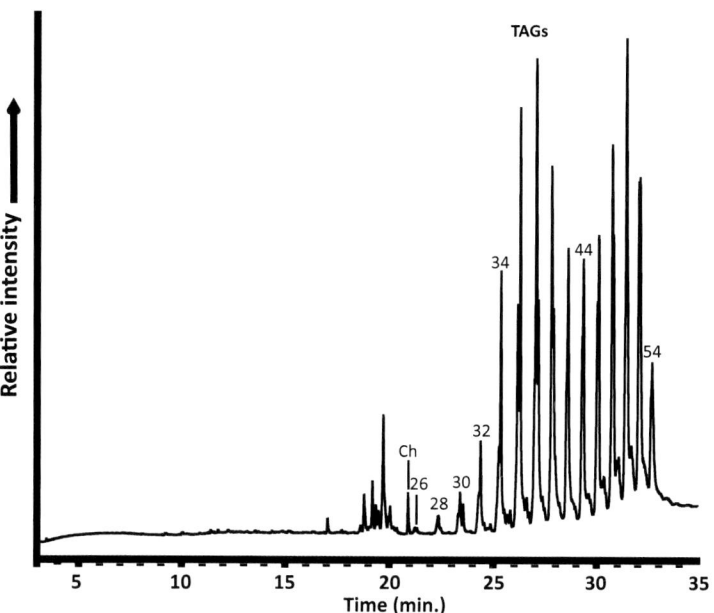

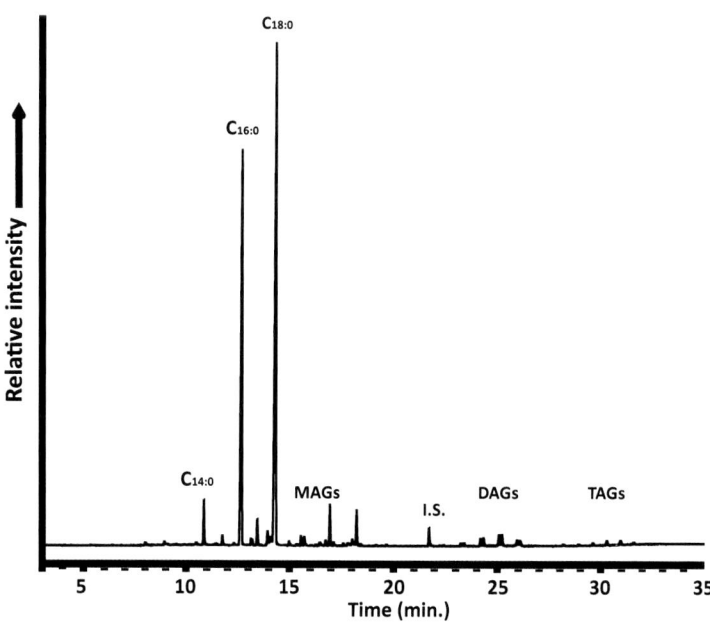

Illus. 7—Gas chromatograms showing the lipid components characteristic of a fresh animal milk fat (top) and a degraded, archaeological fat (bottom). The archaeological example is from potsherd 03E0157:37:36 (BRG-1), part of a Middle Neolithic broad-rimmed vessel from Balregan, Co. Louth. In the lower chromatogram, $Cx:y$ are free fatty acids of carbon length x and degree of unsaturation y. MAGs are monoacylglycerols, DAGs are diacylglycerols and TAGs are triacylglycerols. I.S. is the internal standard (C_{34} n-alkane). In the upper chromatogram (adapted from Salque 2012), numbers are TAGs of carbon length 26–54 and Ch is cholesterol (Jessica Smyth & Richard Evershed).

Further analysing animal fats

Measuring the carbon stable isotope ($\delta^{13}C$) values of individual compounds within a lipid mixture (via GC-combustion-isotope ratio mass spectrometry, or GC-C-IRMS) can provide further information on the origins of pottery lipid residues. In mixtures characteristic of degraded animal fats, $C_{16:0}$ and $C_{18:0}$ free fatty acids tend to dominate (Illus. 7). The $\delta^{13}C$ values of these two fatty acids can be used to distinguish between the animal fats of ruminants (e.g. cattle, sheep and goat) and non-ruminants (such as pig), as differences in the diets of ruminants and non-ruminants and variations in their metabolisms and physiologies result in differences in the $\delta^{13}C$ values of their fats. The different ranges for ruminants and non-ruminants have been verified through experimental work, with a database of carbon stable isotope values carefully generated from modern reference fats, making sure that the diet and environment of reference animals matches prehistoric conditions as closely as possible. The database also includes $\delta^{13}C$ values for marine and freshwater aquatic organisms, broadening the possibilities of assignments still further.

Differences in $\delta^{13}C$ values can also be used to detect dairy fats in archaeological potsherds. In ruminants, the mammary gland is incapable of manufacturing or synthesising the $C_{18:0}$ fatty acid. The $C_{18:0}$ fatty acids in milk fats thus derive from fatty acids 're-routed' from the adipose (meat) fats of the animal, as well as from C_{18} fatty acids taken in directly from the diet. Adipose fats, on the other hand, contain $C_{18:0}$ fatty acids that the animal biosynthesises ultimately and in the main from dietary

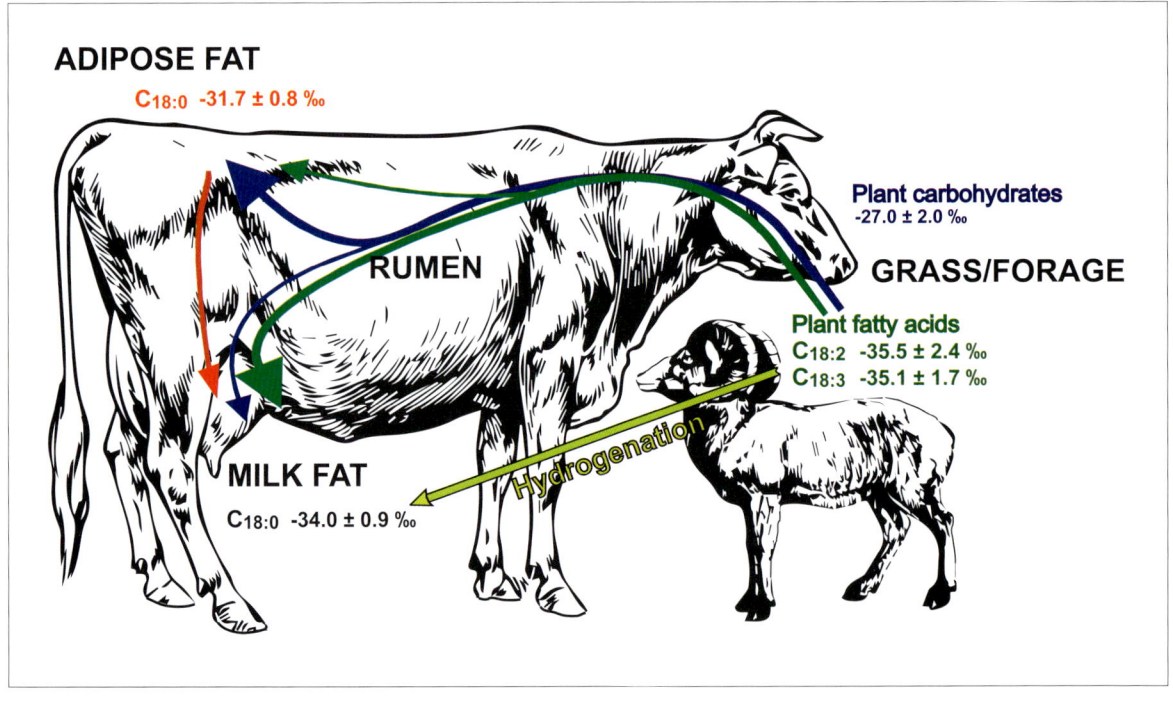

Illus. 8—Diagram showing the routing of dietary fatty acids and carbohydrates in the rumen, adipose tissue and mammary gland of ruminant animals (Jessica Smyth & Richard Evershed).

carbohydrates. Because fatty acids are more depleted in ^{13}C than carbohydrates, the δ^{13}C values of C$_{18:0}$ fatty acids in ruminant dairy fats are c. 2.3‰ lower than in ruminant adipose fats (Illus. 8) (Copley et al. 2003). Again, the verification of this observation, originally made in the field of agricultural science, has required not only a further set of reference values on modern ruminant milks but determinations of the δ^{13}C values of the major fatty acids and carbohydrates of a range of plants representative of the diets of grazing and browsing animals.

Project findings

The SCHERD project examined pottery from three Early Neolithic sites excavated on national road schemes: Magheraboy, Monanny and Kilmainham 1C. The causewayed enclosure at Magheraboy is located on, and just east of, the summit of a prominent ridge on the Cúil Irra peninsula, between the more well-known prominences of Knocknarea, Carrowmore and Carns Hill. Excavation of the eastern half of the monument revealed an incomplete circuit of 10 ditch segments and the slot-trench for an inner timber palisade, which appeared to define a total area of approximately five acres. With the exception of some structural features along the south-western section of the palisade, the excavated portion of the interior contained just 55 pits, scattered across the site in small clusters. Pottery, lithics (chipped stone tools and waste material), cereal remains and burnt bone were recovered from the fills of both the enclosing ditches and the internal pits, and most of this material appeared to derive from distinct episodes of deposition rather than through gradual accumulation during occupation. Pottery was sampled from the pits and the ditches and screened via GC, with 90% of the sherds containing lipid concentrations greater than 5 μg/g. Twenty-three of these absorbed residues were indicative of degraded animal fats. Twenty-two samples were carried forward for compound-specific isotope analysis and all of these produced δ^{13}C values consistent with milk fats (Illus. 9).

At Kilmainham 1C, a large area investigated in advance of the construction of the M3 motorway revealed extensive evidence of activity spanning the Neolithic to medieval periods. Among the remains uncovered were three Early Neolithic post-built structures: Structure 3 was uncovered in the south-west of the site; Structures 1 and 5 lay approximately 70 m to the north-east. A substantial cereal assemblage was recorded from the post-holes of Structure 1, as well as a central hearth, and all three structures were associated with a series of large pits and spreads of occupational debris containing large amounts of ceramic and lithic material. It was these features that were targeted for SCHERD, yielding 23 pottery samples with lipid residues indicative of degraded animal fats. When the δ^{13}C values of the C$_{16:0}$ and C$_{18:0}$ fatty acids from 13 of these samples were determined, results again indicated that milk or milk products were the dominant commodity processed in the pots (Illus. 10).

At Monanny, a cluster of three Early Neolithic buildings (Houses A–C) was uncovered adjacent to a meander on the Longfield River, on a gentle slope sheltered

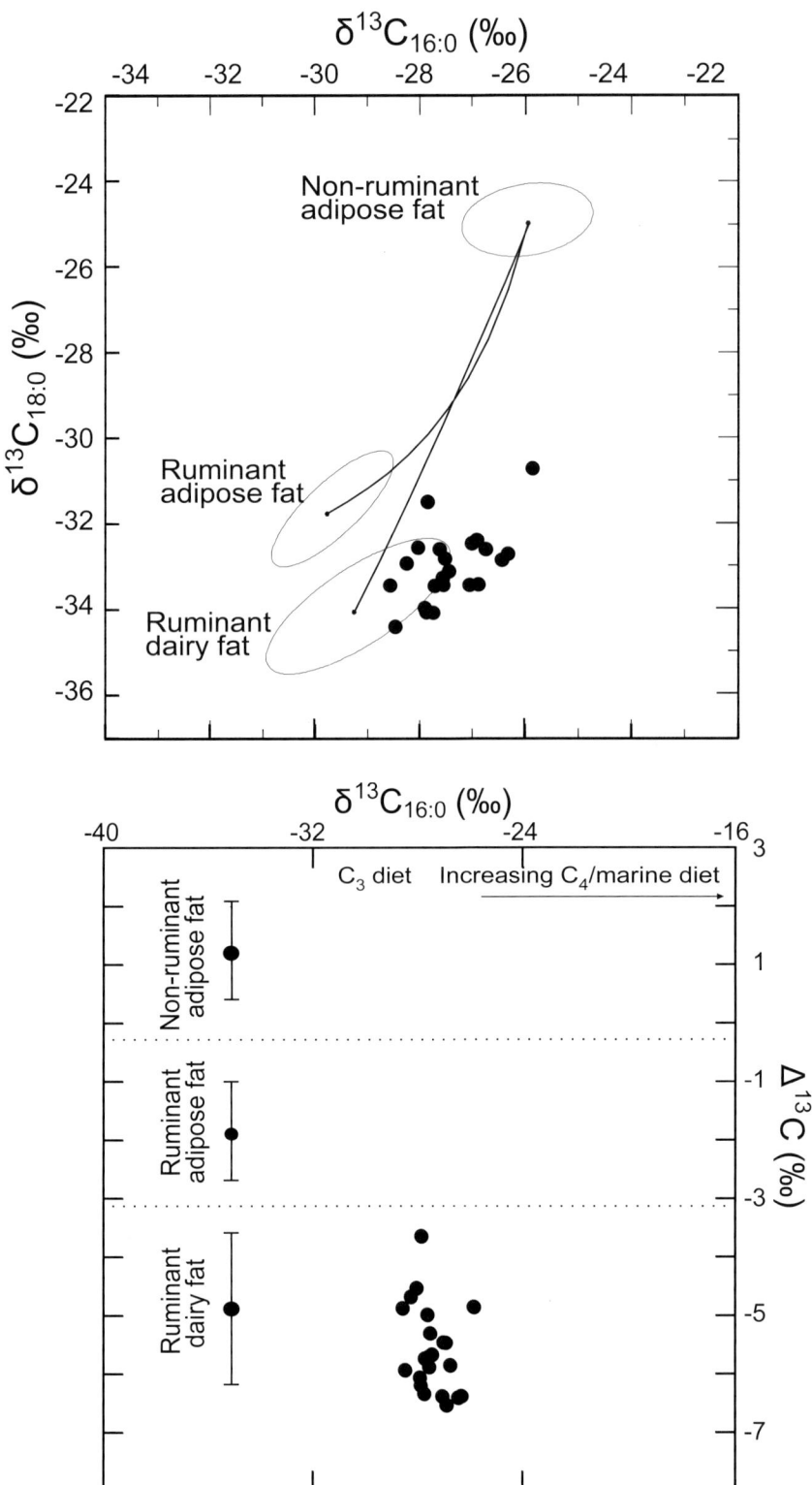

Illus. 9—Top: scatter plot showing $\delta^{13}C$ values of methylated individual fatty acids ($C_{16:0}$ and $C_{18:0}$) from the Magheraboy lipid extracts. These data are plotted against reference ellipses derived from modern UK animal fats that have been corrected for the contribution of post-industrial carbon. Bottom: the same values with $\Delta^{13}C$ values (= $\delta^{13}C_{18:0} - \delta^{13}C_{16:0}$) plotted against $\delta^{13}C_{16:0}$ values. Ranges of the $\Delta^{13}C$ values are based on a global database comprising modern reference animal fats from the UK, Africa, Kazakhstan, Switzerland and the Near East (Jessica Smyth & Richard Evershed).

Milk and molecules: secrets from prehistoric pottery

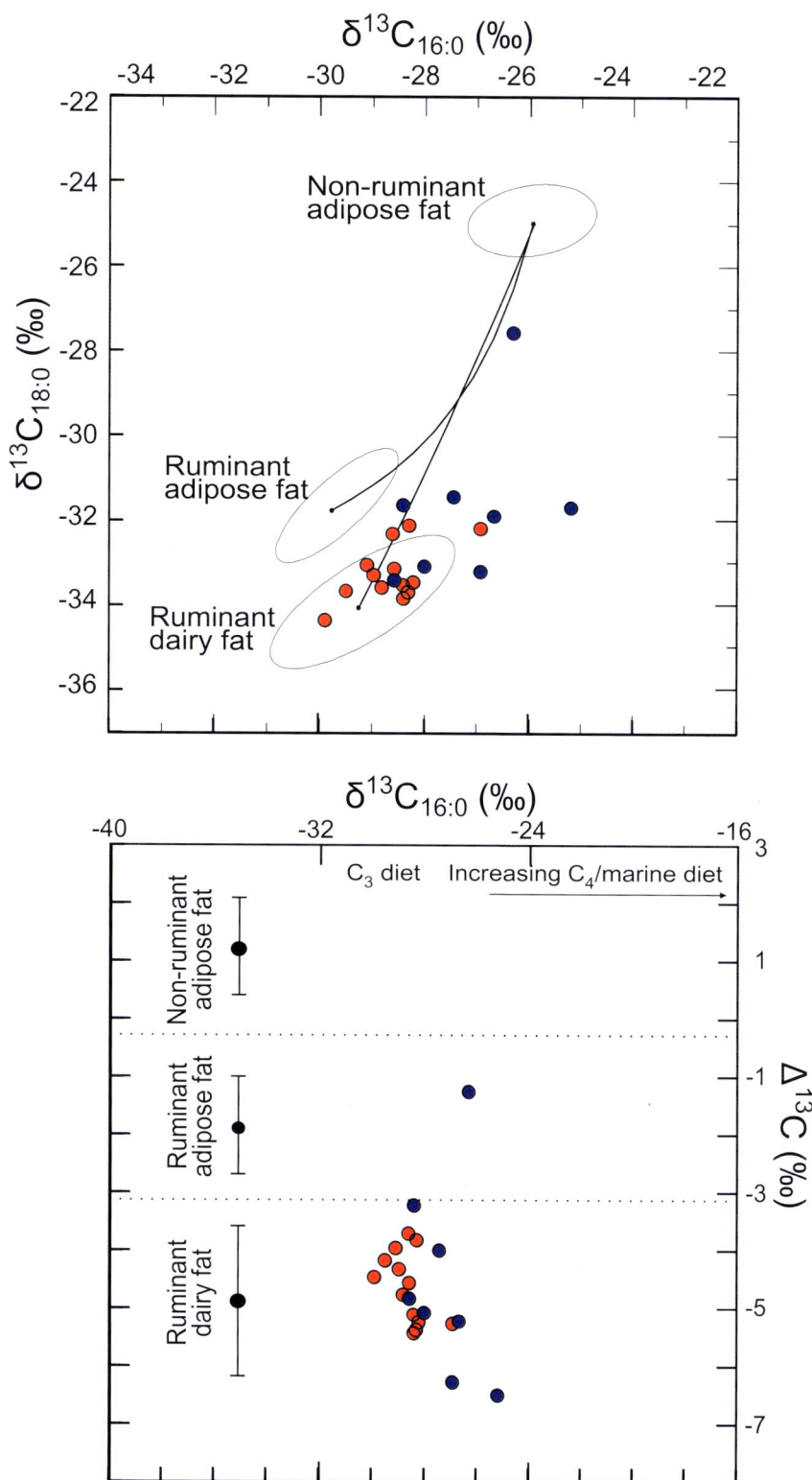

Illus. 10—Top: scatter plot showing δ¹³C values of methylated individual fatty acids ($C_{16:0}$ and $C_{18:0}$) from the Kilmainham 1C (red) and Monanny (blue) lipid extracts. These data are plotted against reference ellipses derived from modern UK animal fats that have been corrected for the contribution of post-industrial carbon. Bottom: the same values with Δ¹³C values (= $δ^{13}C_{18:0} - δ^{13}C_{16:0}$) plotted against $δ^{13}C_{16:0}$ values. Ranges of the Δ¹³C values are based on a global database comprising modern reference animal fats from the UK, Africa, Kazakhstan, Switzerland and the Near East (Jessica Smyth & Richard Evershed).

to the north and west by low drumlins. A small number of isolated pits were also excavated, as well as a possible animal pen or similar ancillary structure north-east of House A and a possible working area immediately north-west of House C. Two of the houses (A and B) had suffered partial damage by fire and were dismantled following abandonment, while House C seems to have completely burnt down. Pottery samples were taken from all three houses and the ancillary structure. Just 10 sherds yielded lipid residues containing the $C_{16:0}$ and $C_{18:0}$ free fatty acids indicative of degraded animal fats, with eight of sufficient concentration to be analysed via GC-C-IRMS. These mostly produced $\delta^{13}C$ values consistent with milk fats, although one sample produced values consistent with meat fats, while another gave values indicative of a mixing of milk and meat fats (Illus. 10).

Lipid analysis and the Early Neolithic

Excitingly, the results of organic residue analysis from sites such as Magheraboy, Kilmainham 1C and Monanny have provided the earliest conclusive evidence for dairying in Ireland, at or around the start of the fourth millennium BC. This is significant for two reasons. First, it tells us that some of the first farming communities on the island were already involved in milking their livestock and processing those products in pots. In other words, dairying was not a farming practice 'discovered' or developed at a later, more advanced stage of agricultural development, what has been referred to as the 'Secondary Products Revolution' (e.g. Sherratt 1981). In Ireland, as far as we can tell, dairying was present from the beginning of the Neolithic (around 3800 BC). Secondly, the ruminant animals that provided this milk—cattle, sheep or goats, or perhaps a combination of all three—were non-native species prior to the Neolithic. They would have had to have been physically shipped, a few animals at a time, over the sea to Ireland (Case 1969). It is thus very likely that the farming groups who ferried across these domesticated animals (and domesticated plants, such as wheat and barley) came equipped with sophisticated knowledge of animal welfare and husbandry. Challenges would have included keeping livestock unstressed and alive during sea crossings, ensuring animals thrived in the new terrain and gradually establishing viable dairy herds.

The results from SCHERD have also highlighted the considerable potential of archaeological lipid analysis for exploring the nature of human–animal relations in the past. The acidity of Irish soils in general does not favour bone preservation. Species identification is often extremely challenging and the construction of kill-off profiles, from which the management of dairy herds is inferred, is near impossible. At Magheraboy, for example, only small quantities of cremated bone fragments from a number of ditch segments and pits survived. These fragments were mainly of sheep/goat, with some larger unidentified mammals also represented. At Kilmainham and Monanny, too, faunal assemblages consisted mostly of small fragments of indeterminate burnt animal bone, occasionally identified as belonging to 'medium-sized' or 'large-sized' mammals. Given these limitations, the identification of ruminant and non-ruminant meat and milk fats on a site can serve as an important proxy for animal exploitation.

This paper hopefully has also demonstrated that lipid analysis is particularly well suited to Irish pottery assemblages. As mentioned above, analysis of several thousand archaeological potsherds over many years has provided a mean lipid yield of c. 100 μg/g. For the potsherds analysed as part of SCHERD, the average lipid yield was 300 μg/g, but in individual sherds was frequently as high as 2–3 mg/g. This may be due to soil acidity, which degrades human and animal bone but seems to preserve lipids particularly well. Indeed, such is the potential for high lipid yields in Irish unglazed vessels (from the Neolithic through to the early medieval period), that statistically robust results can be obtained from fewer than the guideline 30 potsherds. For example, just six pottery sherds from the Neolithic site at Tullahedy, Co. Tipperary, were recently sampled and analysed (Cleary & Kelleher 2011, 387–9), with five sherds yielding traces of degraded animal fats and the carbon stable isotope composition of fatty acids in four of these successfully determined. The pottery from Tullahedy and other sites form part of a very substantial, as yet untapped archaeological resource, and SCHERD is just one example of what can be achieved when cutting-edge science is coupled with archaeological expertise. Similar collaborations are currently mining new molecular-level data from materials such as tooth enamel, human bone and soils. All in all, they point to a very exciting and very fruitful period ahead for biomolecular archaeology in Ireland.

Acknowledgements

The research leading to these results has received funding from the People Programme (Marie Curie Actions) of the European Union's Seventh Framework Programme FP7/2007-2013/ under REA grant agreement No. 273462. The staff of museums, university departments and commercial archaeology companies across Ireland who facilitated access to and sampling of pottery assemblages are warmly thanked, as are colleagues at the Organic Geochemistry Unit at the University of Bristol, who provided help and guidance in the laboratory throughout the Marie Curie fellowship.

2. *'Cad a dhéanfaimid feasta gan adhmad?'* Wooden objects from Irish road schemes
Caitríona Moore

'Cad a dhéanfaimid feasta gan adhmad? Tá deireadh na gcoillte ar lár.'
—Anonymous

'Now what will we do for timber, with the last of the woods laid low?'
—trans. Thomas Kinsella (1981)

These opening lines of the 18th-century Irish song *Cill Chais* lament the decline and sale of Kilcash, Co. Tipperary, and its woods, one of the last great native forests in Ireland (Flood & Flood 1999, 85). The words, by an unknown author, echo a long-standing reverential attitude to trees and the important role they played in ancient Ireland (Kelly 1997, 379; Tierney 1998, 57–8). Wood, which today is almost a luxury material, was in the past used in almost every aspect of daily life: to build shelter and provide fuel for warmth, and to manufacture all sorts of items, from small utensils, such as spoons and bowls, to large composite objects like wheels, carts and pieces of furniture. Despite its ubiquitous use, wood and wooden objects rarely survive in the archaeological record, occurring only when particular environmental conditions prevail, such as a combination of a high water table and a low level of oxygen. When encountered, however, these fragile objects can serve to tell us a great deal. Wooden artefacts provide a wealth of environmental information. Microscopic analysis to identify wood species leads in turn to questions of origin, for example, whether an artefact was likely to have been made from wood growing close to the site or imported from further afield. The analysis of species can also relate to the artefact type and the examination of whether particular types of wood were chosen to make particular types of object and if so, why? The fact that wood was so commonly used for many things, but so rarely survives and is often fragmentary or incomplete, means that these artefacts are sometimes poorly understood. Nonetheless, finds of wooden vessels, tools, agricultural implements and even unidentified objects still provide tantalising glimpses into many aspects of past lives and demonstrate just how important wood was to our ancestors.

Over the course of the last decade several archaeological excavations on national road schemes have uncovered large and well-preserved wooden structures and assemblages of artefacts. These sites include the prehistoric toghers (trackways) of Edercloon, Co. Longford, and Annaholty, Co. Tipperary, and the early medieval horizontal-wheeled watermill at Kilbegly, Co. Roscommon (Illus. 1). Each of these excavations yielded an array of wooden objects, many of which have few, if indeed any, parallels.

Illus. 1—Location of Edercloon, Co. Longford, Kilbegly, Co. Roscommon, and Annaholty, Co. Tipperary (National Roads Authority).

Edercloon

Excavations at Edercloon were directed by the author in the summer of 2006 for CRDS Ltd, in advance of the construction of the N4 Dromod–Roosky Bypass.[1] Edercloon lies just south of the County Leitrim border and is a relatively small townland of 200 hectares, almost half of which is covered by raised bog. The archaeological remains uncovered there lay in a narrow tract of this bog, which, despite recent drainage and reclamation, contained an exceptionally well-preserved complex of wooden trackways and platforms and other deposits of worked wood. The Edercloon complex is extraordinary for many reasons and, spanning from the Neolithic to the early medieval period, was clearly a place of some significance in the

---

[1] NGR 206861, 285027; height 25 m OD; Excavation Reg. No. E3313; Ministerial Direction No. A031.

past (Moore 2008, 1–12; McDermott et al. 2009, 49–64). The toghers of Edercloon ranged from simple paths laid to cross short, perhaps treacherous sections of the bog, to very large multiphase structures maintained over centuries and created to access the wider landscape surrounding Edercloon. Many of these sites avoided the adjacent dryland and instead appear to have provided routeways within and through the wetlands. This was particularly the case in the centuries of the Late Bronze Age (1100–800 BC) and Iron Age (800 BC–AD 400), when several very large toghers were joined together to create a network of interconnected paths and platforms. It was during this time that wooden artefacts began to be deposited at Edercloon, in what was clearly a structured and deliberate manner (Moore 2009a). Forty-six wooden objects were found, including fragments of prehistoric wheels, finely pointed spears, tool handles, vessels and many items of indeterminate function. Wooden vessels were one of the most common find types, with two particularly fine examples providing a wealth of information about how they were manufactured and used.

A fragment of an alder vessel was found in the base of EDC 26, an Iron Age trackway radiocarbon-dated to 390–170 BC (Lab code Wk-20201; see O'Sullivan & Stanley (2008, 164) for full details) (Illus. 2). Alder is a small, scrubby tree that grows well in damp conditions and is to be found around the edges of bogs and alongside

Illus. 2—A fragment of an alder bowl being excavated from the Iron Age togher EDC 26 at Edercloon, Co. Longford (CRDS Ltd).

rivers and lakes (Stuijts 2005, 139). In early Irish law alder was listed as a 'commoner of the wood', meaning that it was of lesser economic value than certain other species (Kelly 1997, 380). Folklore beliefs associated with alder trees are generally negative, possibly due to the fact that when cut, the timber changes from white to vivid red, reminiscent of blood (Nelson & Walsh 1993, 49). Despite this, alder was a very useful tree. It was easily carved and was commonly selected for the manufacture of objects, particularly vessels, but also wheels and shields (ibid., 50). The selection of alder for the manufacture of wooden vessels, especially those made to contain liquid, was quite deliberate. Alder, being a damp species, retains liquids well and does not impart any flavour to foodstuffs (Taylor 1981, 45). The vessel fragment from EDC 26 is approximately half of a carved oblong bowl, which was broken prior to its inclusion in the togher. The bowl appears to have been well used, with much of its outer surface and rim displaying evidence of wear and damage. The inner surface has suffered even more, it is not only worn but also scorched in several places (Illus. 3). Measuring just over 500 mm in length, this was a very large vessel and as such was probably used during communal mealtimes. It is easy to picture it filled with all manner of foodstuffs—cheese, fruit or meat—and being passed around a large gathering of people, perhaps on occasion coming too close to the embers of the fire. Being so obviously worn, it seems likely that this was an everyday item and one that certainly received heavy and repeated use.

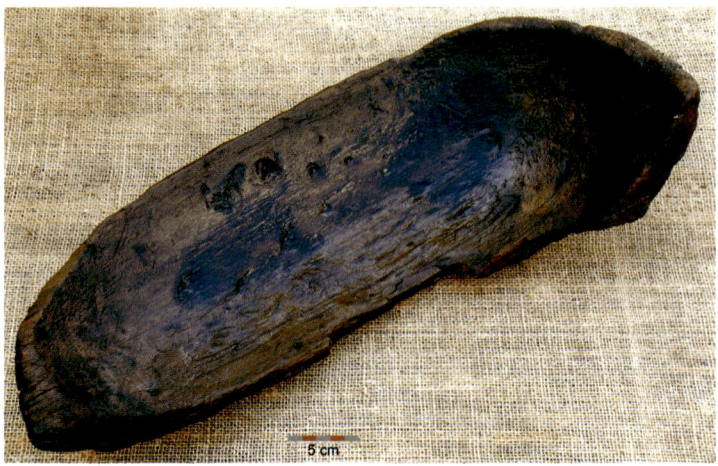

Illus. 3—The worn and scorched surfaces and rim of the Iron Age alder bowl (John Sunderland).

A second vessel from Edercloon is of much finer manufacture and may have been a special and carefully kept possession. This vessel was found in EDC 49, an early medieval togher radiocarbon-dated to AD 680–880 (Wk-25203; see Stanley et al. (2010, 119) for full details). It too was carved from alder, the preference for which was demonstrated by its selection to make eight of the nine vessels found at Edercloon, one of which is represented only by a lid. The EDC 49 dish was broken into 17 pieces and scattered at two locations in the togher. It is almost complete and, like the EDC 26 bowl, shows some signs of use before its deposition in the site. The inner surface is worn and smooth in contrast to the base and outer sides, which are covered in very fine, crisp toolmarks of a sharp blade, probably a chisel (Illus. 4). These bands of toolmarks, while being a by-product of the manufacturing process, are also likely to be a simple decorative motif. The disparity in preservation between the inside and outside of the dish may be due to how it was stored. At each end is an exquisitely carved lozenge-shaped handle (Illus. 5). The handles are both perforated with small holes, one at one end and two at the opposite end. These perforations are quite heavily worn and both are broken. This suggests that they were functional, so perhaps this vessel was suspended for the safe-keeping of the object itself, or maybe the items it generally contained required it to be used in this way. Measuring almost 600 mm in length, this dish, like that from EDC 26, is very large and was likely used for communal eating, perhaps reserved for special occasions, such as feasts.

These two wooden dishes are objects with which we can identify today and it is quite easy to understand and picture how they were used in the past. This is not so in the case of six small objects found in two toghers at Edercloon. Each object comprised a hazel rod around which a second stem had been trained to grow, the two components fusing together to create a spiral shape (Illus. 6). In three instances the outer stem was subsequently removed, leaving only a shallow indentation around the central stem. In the remaining three artefacts the outer stem is still in place. These objects were recovered from Iron Age trackway EDC 26 (see above) and Bronze Age EDC 5, a large togher dendrochronologically dated to 1120 BC ± 9 years or later (Q11026; see Kelly et al. (2013, 136) for full details) and radiocarbon-dated to 1260–970 BC (Wk-20961; see O'Sullivan & Stanley (2008, 164) for full details).[2]

Pieces of hazel or willow similar in appearance to these objects sometimes occur naturally when creepers such as honeysuckle wind themselves around trees, squeezing the branches and creating a spiral pattern. It is possible that such pieces provided inspiration for the Edercloon artefacts, which were trained and took four to seven years to grow (I Stuijts, pers. comm.). The training and harvesting of these rods may have coincided with a cycle of coppicing. Coppicing is a traditional method of woodland management whereby certain tree species, hazel in particular, are cut to a stump to encourage new growth of long, straight branches, often in a four- or seven-year cycle (Stuijts 2005, 151). Ranging from 990 mm to 2410 mm in length and 110 mm to 300 mm in diameter, all of these artefacts were broken prior to

---

[2] The correct calibrated radiocarbon date for EDC 5 is 1260–970 BC, but it has been published incorrectly elsewhere as 1206–970 BC.

Fragments of Lives Past

Illus. 4—The exquisitely carved alder dish from early medieval togher EDC 49. Its inner surface is smooth and worn while its outer sides are covered in fine toolmarks (John Sunderland).

'Cad a dhéanfaimid feasta gan adhmad?' Wooden objects from Irish road schemes

Illus. 5—The carefully carved and perforated lozenge-shaped handles (John Sunderland).

deposition, but several have evidence of having been worked along their length or, in one case, a carefully trimmed end (Illus. 7). These hazel rods are highly ornamental and it is suggested that they may have functioned as the decorative upper portions of walking sticks or staffs and originally may have been up to 1,500 mm in length. With only one parallel in the archaeological record (see below), an exact function for these pieces remains unknown, although clues may lie with the fact that they were made from hazel.

Hazel is generally a small, bushy tree that grows in a variety of geographical locations, although it does not like wet conditions (Stuijts 2005, 140). In ancient Ireland, hazel was considered a 'noble of the wood'. It was economically valuable, being prized for its fast-growing, pliable rods that were used for weaving wattle, hurdles and baskets. Hazel trees were also an important source of food, with hazel nuts providing a precious supply of fat and protein (Kelly 1997, 380–82). In Irish folklore hazel was the tree of wisdom (Nelson & Walsh 1993, 71) and hazel wands, in particular, were associated with the inauguration of kings (Simms 1987, 23). To this end, it is interesting to speculate that the six trained hazel rods from Edercloon were special objects, chosen specifically for burial within the toghers. These items could quite easily have been carved from larger branches of wood, but instead were deliberately and slowly trained into these shapes. The inclusion of artefacts in the toghers of Edercloon was a highly structured activity and the assemblage as a whole strongly indicates a ritual aspect to the site (Moore 2009a). Interestingly, a similar piece of hazel was recovered from the Iron Age togher at Annaholty, Co. Tipperary (see below and Moore 2009b), strengthening the idea that these pieces of wood were purposely selected for inclusion in these sites.

Annaholty

Excavations at Annaholty were directed by Kate Taylor for TVAS (Ireland) Ltd in 2007, in advance of the construction of the N7 Nenagh–Limerick High Quality Dual Carriageway. The site consisted of a very large timber trackway that crossed a narrow tract of raised bog between two dryland islands (Taylor 2008, 55).[3] It was dendrochronologically dated to around 40 BC (ibid.; Kelly et al. 2013, 136) and although different from the Edercloon trackways in many ways, it did produce an assemblage of wooden artefacts buried in two locations underneath the trackway. The Annaholty artefact assemblage included vessel fragments, possible cart pieces and a fragment of an animal yoke (Illus. 8) (Taylor 2010, 8–9). The animal yoke was carved from ash, which, like hazel, was a 'noble of the wood' and was highly prized in the past for its use in the manufacture of furniture and spear shafts (Kelly 1997, 383). Ash also held a special place in Irish folklore, with ancient ash trees being venerated and often associated with significant sites, such as at St Brigid's

---

[3] NGR 168385, 163535; height 45 m OD; Excavation Reg. No. E3530; Ministerial Direction No. A026.

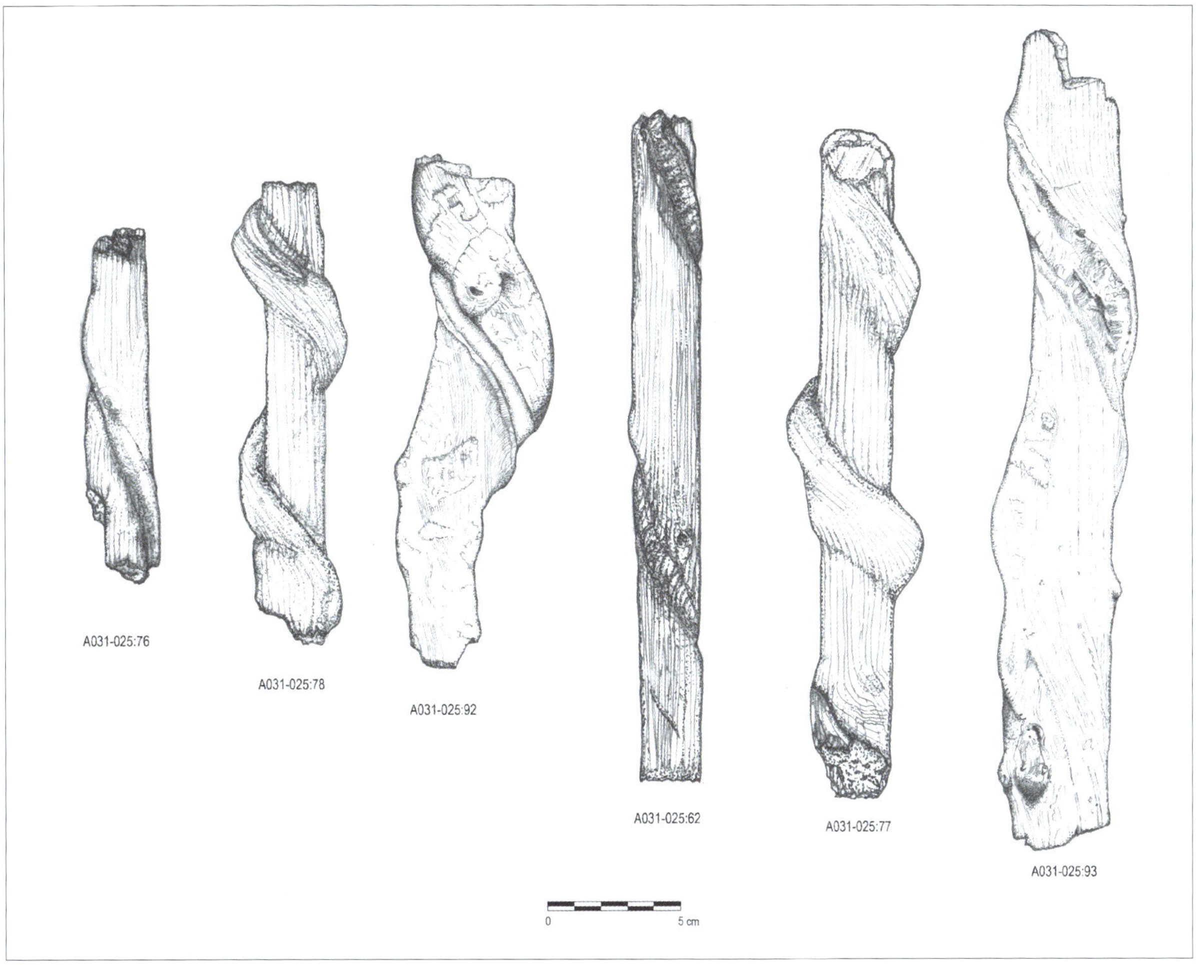

Illus. 6—The six trained hazel brushwood fragments from EDC 5 and EDC 26 (Drawings by Marianna Ripa & Eamon Russell, CRDS Ltd).

Illus. 7—The trained hazel rod (Find no. A031-025:77) with the carefully trimmed end from Bronze Age togher EDC 5 (John Sunderland).

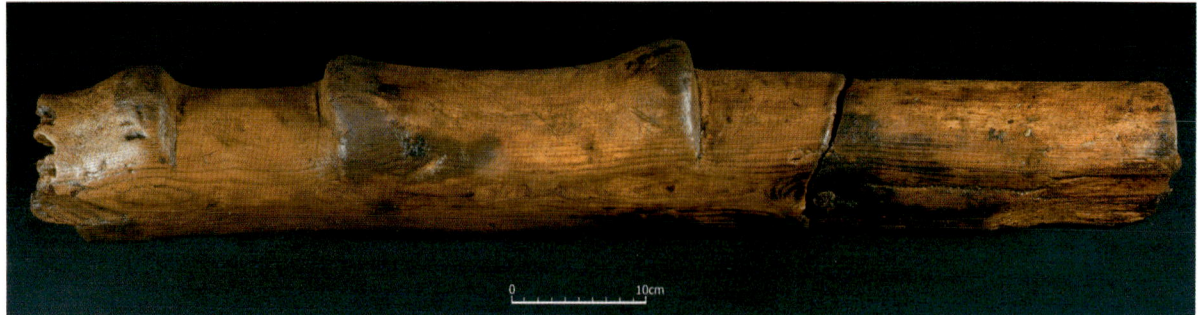

Illus. 8—The carved ash head yoke from Annaholty, Co. Tipperary (John Sunderland).

Cathedral in County Kildare (Nelson & Walsh 1993, 139). Ash wood is strong and elastic, making it an obvious choice for an item such as a yoke, which would have been subject to continuous and repetitive movement. Once again this demonstrates the deliberate choice of an appropriate wood species to create a particular object. The Annaholty yoke is part of a head yoke and would have been placed behind the horns of an animal and attached by means of straps. Head yokes may date from as early as 2000 BC in mainland Europe, and are likely to be among the earliest devices created to use animals for draught (Fenton 1986, 37). The Annaholty fragment is incomplete and its surfaces are worn and smooth, suggesting it was used prior to its deposition in the togher. Recent research into the deposition of artefacts in Irish bogs has proposed that items associated with transport and bridlery are, like the twisted hazel rods above, associated with kings and inauguration (Kelly 2006, 26–30). While the Annaholty artefacts may be part of this wider tradition, the yoke is also rare early evidence for the harnessing of animals in draught in order to cultivate the land or to pull a cart.

Kilbegly

Excavations at Kilbegly, directed by Neil Jackman for Valerie J Keeley Ltd, were undertaken in 2007 in advance of the construction of the M6 Ballinasloe–Athlone Motorway. Discovered in a shallow peat basin in this small corner of County Roscommon was an exceptionally well-preserved, horizontal-wheeled watermill, one of the finest examples of its type discovered in Europe.[4] Radiocarbon dates indicate that it was built and used within the period of the seventh to ninth centuries AD (Jackman 2013, 40). The structural remains of the mill were made entirely of wood and, not surprisingly, the site contained a large assemblage of wooden artefacts. Most of these are simple items associated with the mill buildings and mechanisms, things like pegs, a rope of slender twigs known as a withy, pulleys and parts of the millwheel and paddles. The majority of the artefacts are heavily worn and eroded,

---

[4] NGR 190038, 230053; height 49 m OD; Excavation Reg. No. E3369; Ministerial Direction No. A034.

reflecting the industrial nature of the site. The dominant wood species identified at Kilbegly was oak, which was used in both the structure of the mill and to make almost half of the 99 wooden artefacts recovered there (O Carroll 2013, 57–60). In ancient Irish law oak (*dair* in Irish) was a 'noble of the wood', economically valued for its acorns, which were used as fodder, and the provision of large timbers for buildings and other large-scale wood-working (Kelly 1997, 380–81). More than any other tree, the importance of oak in Ireland can be seen in the numerous place-names of which it is a component in the form of 'derry' (e.g. Edenderry, Derrynaflan, etc.).

One of the most interesting artefacts from Kilbegly was a complete oak spade (Illus. 9), discovered in the tail-race of the mill (Moore 2013, 56). It is carved from a single piece of oak and has a very slightly dished blade (Illus. 10). This is a very early form of spade with a distinctive one-sided design, directly related to whether the user was right- or left-footed (Evans 1957, 132). On a busy, industrious site, such as an early medieval mill, this would have been a very useful tool, used daily for shovelling grain or for clearance and maintenance of the mill structure and water channels. Found buried within the fills of the tail-race channel, the Kilbegly spade may have been abandoned along with the site, but given how useful a tool it was, it seems more likely that it was lost, perhaps accidentally dropped and washed downstream in a rush of water through the mill.

Conclusion

This small selection of wooden artefacts from NRA-funded excavations has taken us from the centuries of the Late Bronze Age and Iron Age through to the early medieval period. Overall they are quite simple objects, yet they have imparted a great deal of information about how past peoples exploited trees to create all manner of items, from the practical to the aesthetic. Trees were chosen for their individual

Illus. 9—The front (top) and back of the oak spade found in the tail-race of the early medieval watermill at Kilbegly, Co. Roscommon (John Sunderland).

Illus. 10—Detail of the front of the complete oak spade, showing the slightly concave blade (John Sunderland).

characteristics, ideally suited to the objects they were destined to become. Beyond knowing that hurleys are carved from ash, such knowledge of woods and woodcraft is sadly foreign to most people today. Through these artefacts we have been offered glimpses into aspects of daily life ranging from the mundane to the spiritual. We have visited with prehistoric and medieval families as they shared a meal and seen how the burial and sometimes manufacture of objects may have been part of religious or sacred activities. On a somewhat more prosaic level, we have seen evidence of how our ancestors strove to harness animals, cultivate the soil and process its bounty. This collection of items has ably demonstrated just how ubiquitous and important wood was in the past and how much knowledge we are missing in its frequent absence from the archaeological record.

Acknowledgements

The author would like to thank the NRA for the opportunity to participate in the seminar and to contribute to this publication. Thanks also to Kate Taylor of TVAS (Ireland) Ltd and Neil Jackman of Abarta Audio Guides.

3. The people behind the pots: considering the Early Bronze Age remains from French Furze, Tully East, Co. Kildare

Ros Ó Maoldúin

Investigations undertaken in 2002, in advance of the construction of the M7 Kildare Bypass, led to the discovery of a small, unenclosed, Early Bronze Age settlement at French Furze, Tully East townland, Co. Kildare.[1] Among the artefacts found on the site were six sherds of decorated 'bowl tradition' pottery. While those few potsherds may appear quite paltry, the information they reveal about the people who lived at the site and the contribution they can make to our wider knowledge of life during the Early Bronze Age in Ireland is perhaps more significant than at first expected—especially when viewed in the context of other sites and finds from the local region and further afield.

Bowl tradition pottery gets its name from the bowl shape of a short and squat type of pot most commonly found accompanying Early Bronze Age human burials. When found with burials, the pots are often complete (Illus. 1) and range from 8 cm to 15 cm in height (Ó Ríordáin & Waddell 1993). Finds from a domestic context

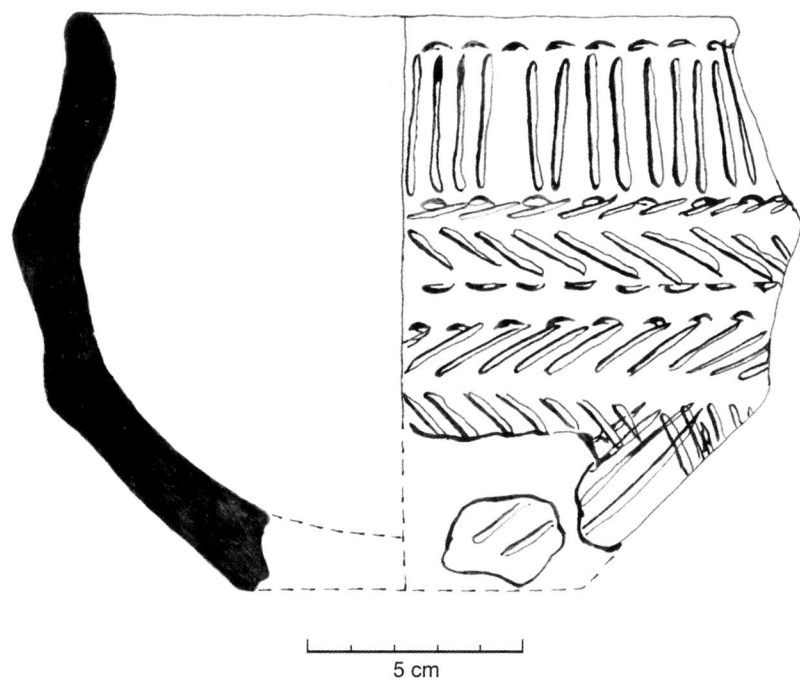

Illus. 1—An unprovenanced bowl tradition pot of the type found accompanying burials (after Ó Ríordáin & Waddell 1993).

---

[1] NGR 274080, 211778; height 92 m OD; Excavation Licence No. 02E0541.

are rare and are found only as broken sherds. They are connected with the funerary pottery on the basis of decorative comparisons and appear to have included a wider range of shapes and sizes (Waddell 2010, 154). The occurrence of this pottery type at French Furze provides us with an important link between the community who lived there and the bowl tradition burials within the region, and from this we can infer widespread social connections with groups using similarly decorated pottery elsewhere. It also provides an opportunity to examine contemporary practice in a domestic context and consider what this might reveal about the distinctive way in which a Bronze Age community viewed and interacted with their world.

The site

The settlement (designated Site 11) was in an area known locally as French Furze, off Frenchfurze Road, in the townland of Tully East. This is approximately 1 km south-east of the centre of Kildare Town, on the north-western edge of the extensive open plains of common land known as The Curragh (Illus. 2). The excavation was carried out by the author for Valerie J Keeley Ltd, on behalf of the NRA and Kildare County Council.

Illus. 2—Location of Site 11 at French Furze, Tully East, Co. Kildare (based on the Ordnance Survey Ireland Discovery Series map).

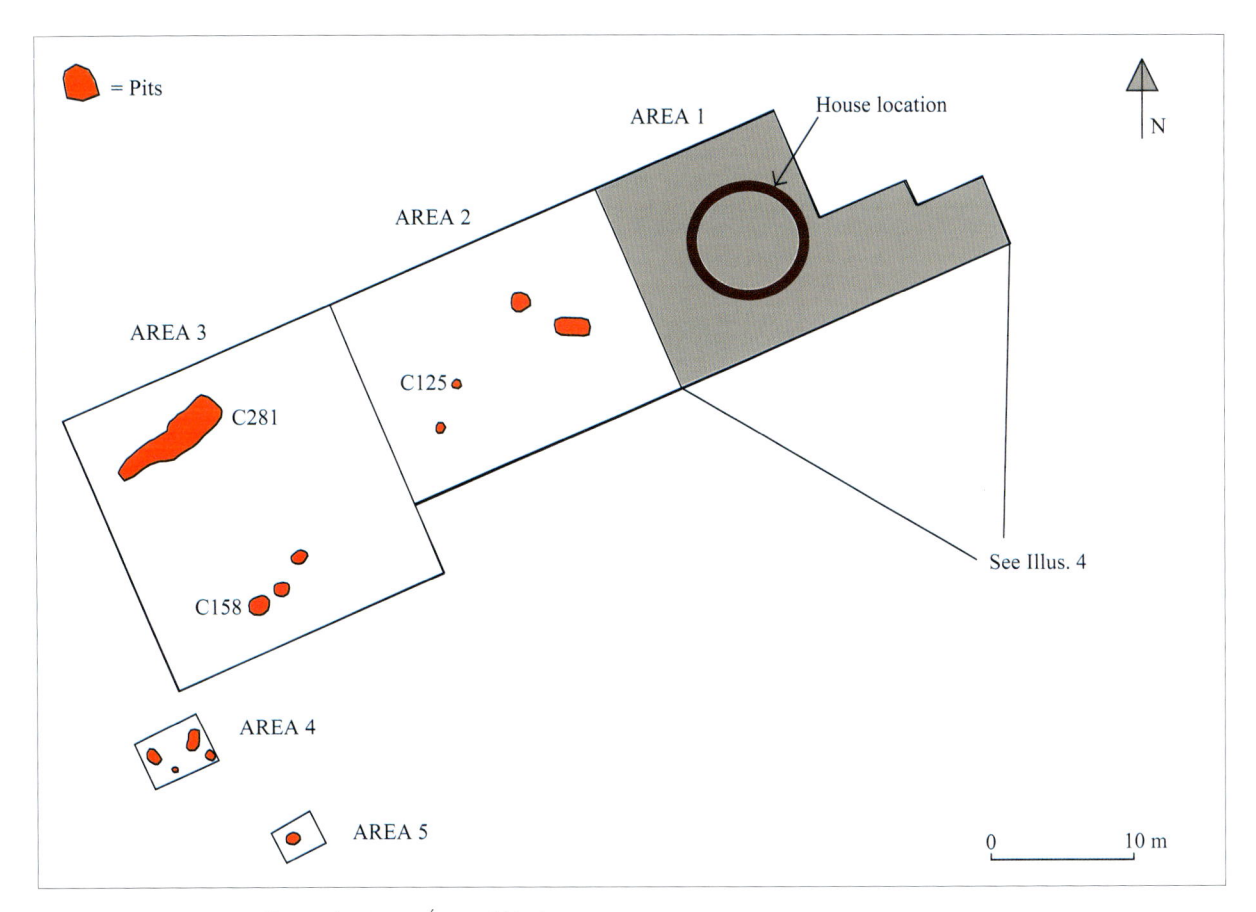

Illus. 3—Overall site plan (Ros Ó Maoldúin).

The archaeological remains comprised a scatter of pits, post-holes, stake-holes and hearths, on a south-facing slope a short distance north of a small stream (Illus. 3). Many of these features were truncated by modern cultivation furrows. The post- and stake-holes and the hearths formed a cluster in the eastern end of the site (Area 1). Structural outlines were not easily discernible (Illus. 4), but they are likely to represent the remains of one or more houses and associated animal pens (a possible reconstruction is discussed below). The pits were concentrated in the west of the site, between c. 15 m and 50 m away from the structural remains. Some of those closer to the house structures appear to have contained deposits of domestic waste, while those further down the slope predominantly contained fire-cracked stone and charcoal. The latter pits were most likely used to heat water, possibly to steam-cook food.

Pottery and lithics (chipped stone tools and waste material) were discovered in several of the cut features and additional lithics were retrieved from the ploughsoil overlying these. The lithics are predominantly flint, but also include a few pieces of chert, and were likely worked from pebbles found in local glacial deposits. The assemblage includes seven retouched scrapers (both end and side scrapers) and is characteristic of a later prehistoric date. The pottery is all of the Early Bronze Age bowl tradition and, according to Brindley's (2007) typo-chronology (dating scheme),

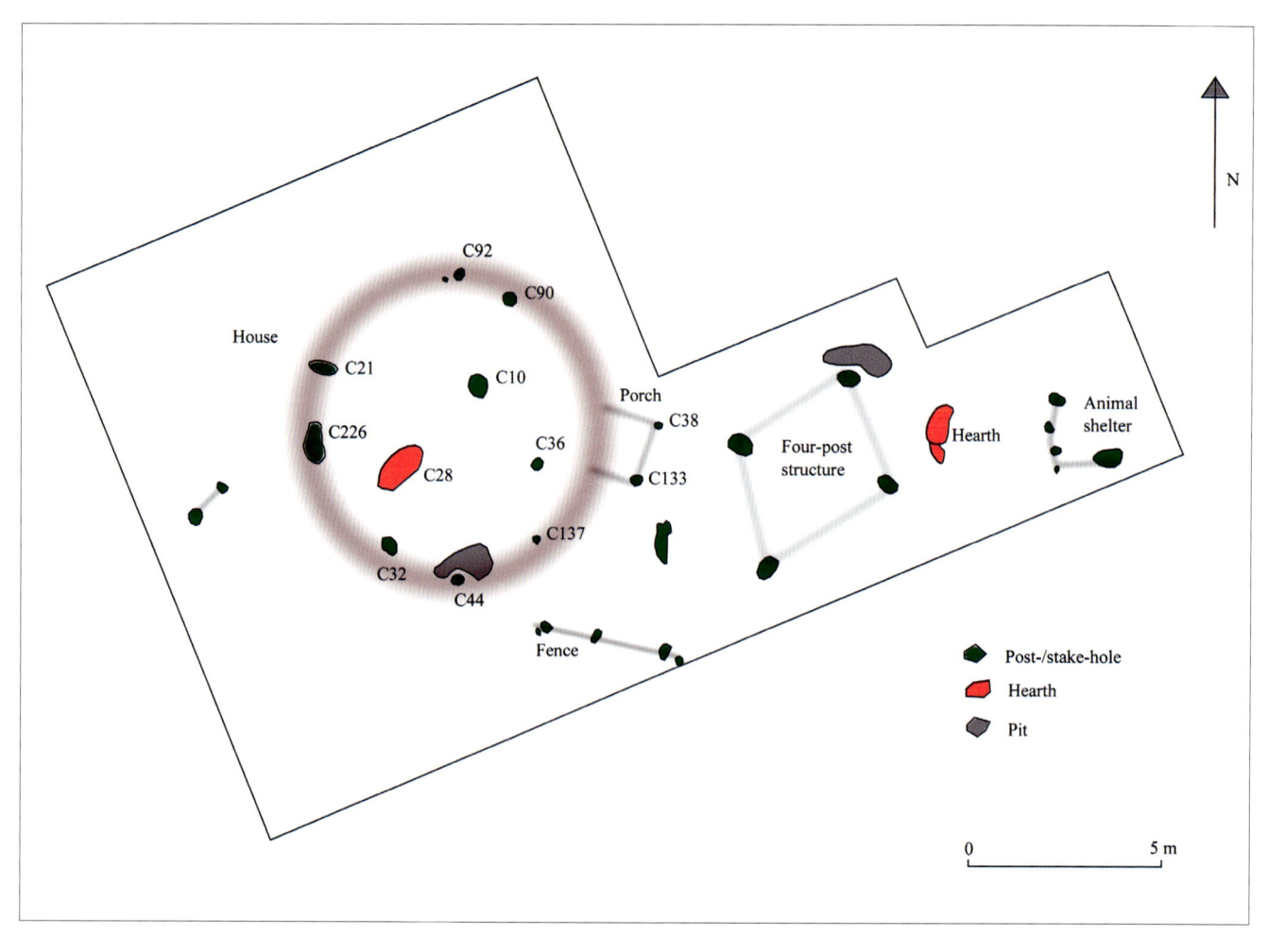

Illus. 4—Plan of eastern feature cluster, with possible structural outlines indicated (Ros Ó Maoldúin).

dates from between 2160 BC and 1930/20 BC. It was found in two features: a post-hole (C133) in the structural cluster in the east of the site (Illus. 4); and a pit (C125) c. 15 m west of this (Illus. 3). No animal bones were found on the site, but this is likely to be due to the acidity of the soil dissolving them.

Environmental samples from two pits (C158 and C281) in the west of the site (Area 3) contained charred cereal grains, including probable free-threshing wheat, grass seeds and pulse fragments, and a mixture of hazel, apple-type, plum-type, ash and hawthorn or mountain ash charcoal. The charred grains and pulse fragments suggest that the material in the pits included food waste. The combination of tree species represented in the charcoal suggests a relatively dry landscape, with a mixture of open and wooded areas. A sample of the charcoal from the upper fill of pit C158 was radiocarbon-dated to 2140–1880 BC (SUERC-6760; see Appendix 1 for details). While only one radiocarbon date was commissioned from French Furze, the complementary date of the pottery found in two other features (pit C125 and post-hole C133, see below) affords the site a degree of temporal cohesion.

Illus. 5—Artist's reconstruction of Early Bronze Age life at French Furze (JG O'Donoghue).

It is difficult to discern a definitive structural outline among the post- and stake-holes at French Furze; however, a number of rings or arcs can be suggested (Illus. 4) and one possible reconstruction based on those remains, worked out in collaboration with heritage artist JG O'Donoghue, is presented above (Illus. 5). It is proposed that a ring created by six post-holes (C137, C44, C226, C21 C92 and C90), with two internal supports (C36 and C10), an internal hearth (C28) and a possible porch feature (C133 and C38), formed the most convincing structural outline. This possible outline suggests a circular structure c. 6.5 m in diameter, with a small porch orientated to the south-east. Beyond this may have been an area that was partly delineated by a fence line, where people could have kept small livestock in pens, knapped lithics around external hearths and undertook other daily tasks. Four post-holes in this area may represent the remains of a grain storage platform, but this was not included in the reconstruction. An additional pair of post-holes (C218 and C183) to the rear of the proposed house structure could have supported a rack, perhaps for drying or tanning hides.

Circular houses predominated throughout most of Irish prehistory, except for a period during the Early Neolithic, and the postulated house design is not dissimilar to others more clearly represented elsewhere, such as Ballyveelish, Co. Tipperary (Doody

1988). In an ongoing review of the Irish Bronze Age, archaeologist Charles Mount (pers. comm.) has identified 87 Early Bronze Age structures from 41 settlements, several of which have identifiable porches; he believes the porches may be a mark of social status.

The pottery and the contexts of its discovery

The pottery from French Furze was identified and analysed by prehistoric pottery expert Anna Brindley. It included one very well-preserved sherd (Find no. 02E0541:5; Illus. 6) and five less well-preserved sherds (Illus. 7). The well-preserved sherd was from the body of a large vessel that exhibited an internal angle and two low applied ridges, or cordons, on its exterior, above and below the shoulder. Its surfaces were well finished and alternating bands of incised oblique lines decorated the exterior. The sherd was discovered placed upright in the post-hole (C133) interpreted as the southern support of the house porch (Illus. 8), i.e. the left-hand post as one entered the building. The evidence suggests that the wooden post decomposed within the post-hole so the potsherd must have been placed here before the post was inserted. The fact that the only sherd found in a post-hole, or anywhere around the house, came from a probable porch support may be particularly significant. Entrances are liminal spaces—places between, neither inside or out—and cross-culturally are commonly marked by ritual. There are many examples of this; perhaps those most familiar in Ireland are how people bless themselves at the entrance to a church or hang a horseshoe above a door. What interests us here, however, is what is distinctive about the Bronze Age form of this ritual, and the object itself may reveal something. It is likely to have been a 'foundation deposit', deliberately placed in a ritual act that perhaps sought to confer good fortune upon the house-dwellers.

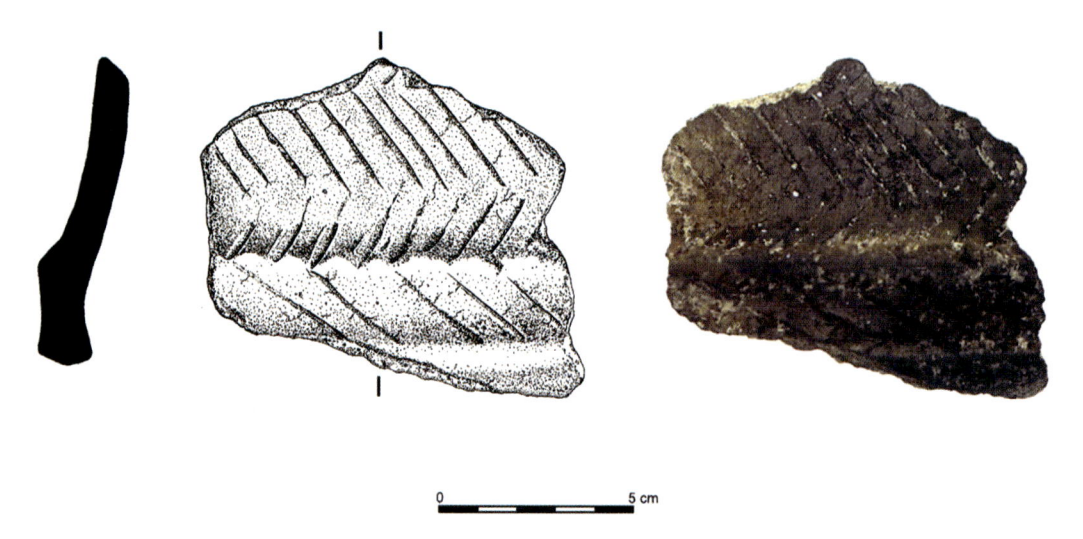

Illus. 6—The well-preserved, bowl tradition potsherd (02E0541:5) from post-hole C133 in Area 1 (Valerie J Keeley Ltd).

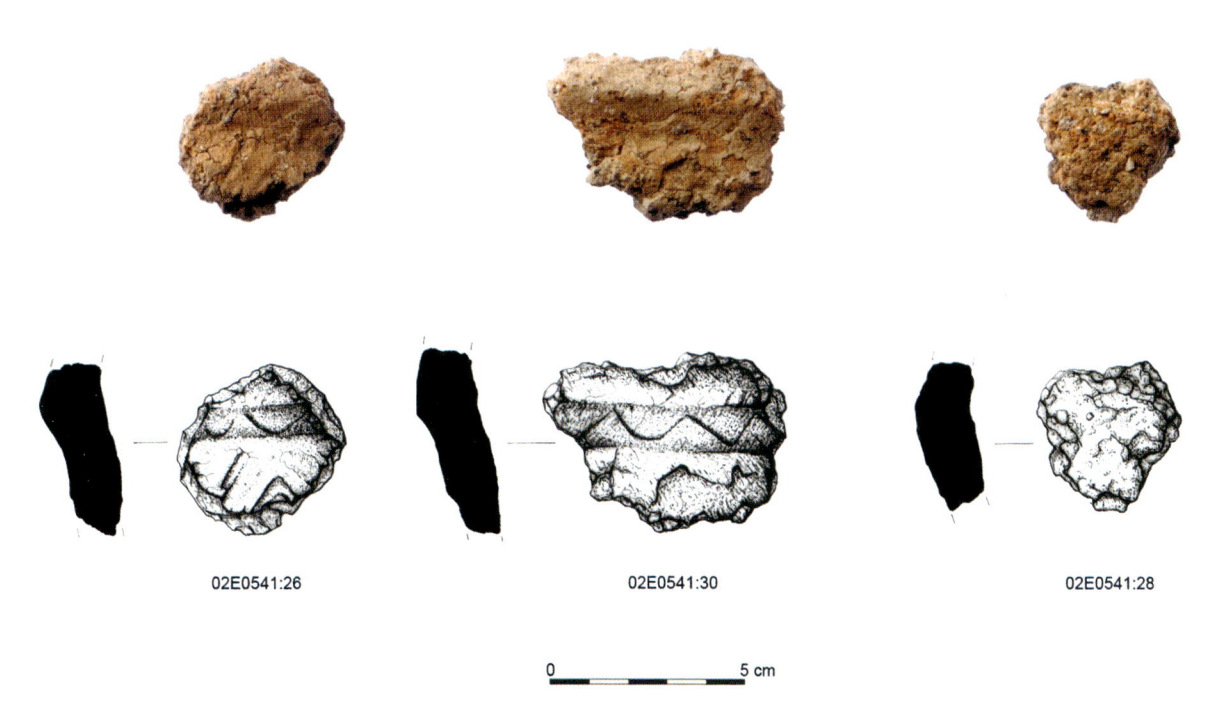

The people behind the pots

Illus. 7—Three of the less well-preserved, bowl tradition potsherds from pit C125 in Area 2 (Valerie J Keeley Ltd).

Illus. 8—The well-preserved potsherd as found in post-hole C133 (Valerie J Keeley Ltd).

Although it was a particularly well-preserved sherd, its edges were relatively abraded. Perhaps the vessel from which it came had been broken some time ago and the potsherd had been regularly handled over a prolonged period before its deposition? Assuming it was used as a foundation deposit, we might imagine that it was a fragment of pot used during the life of a previous house, at this site or possibly at an earlier settlement, from which the community at French Furze had moved; its deposition may have established a connection with such a past structure or place.

The five less well-preserved fragments were from the primary fill (C136) of pit C125 (Illus. 9), c. 15 m to the rear, or south-west, of the structure. Although more fragmentary, the presence of a low applied cordon, a shoulder and decoration made it possible to identify the sherds as bowl tradition pottery from a single vessel similar to that to which the better preserved sherd belonged. The decoration comprised triangular impressions on the cordon and traces of shallow grooved lines.

While there can be practical reasons to dispose of refuse in a certain way, the manner in which communities carry it out is often highly culturally circumscribed (Moore 1986, 102–6), involving concepts of pollution, purity and taboo (Douglas 1966). In Hodder's (1982) comparative study of different Nuba groups in Sudan, he convincingly showed how ideology was a major factor in determining different patterns of disposal. Viewing the deposition of the French Furze sherds as the disposal of 'refuse' from a modern Western or purely materialist vantage-point may be a mistake (Brück 2006, 300–301). To do so is to rely on our own world view as the main source of analogy, when there are arguably much better, or at least broader, perspectives available, particularly from ethnoarchaeological studies (David & Kramer 2001). As such, the positioning of the pit to the rear and at some remove from the house may indicate a ritual necessity to separate this disposal from the immediate area or view of the front of the structure.

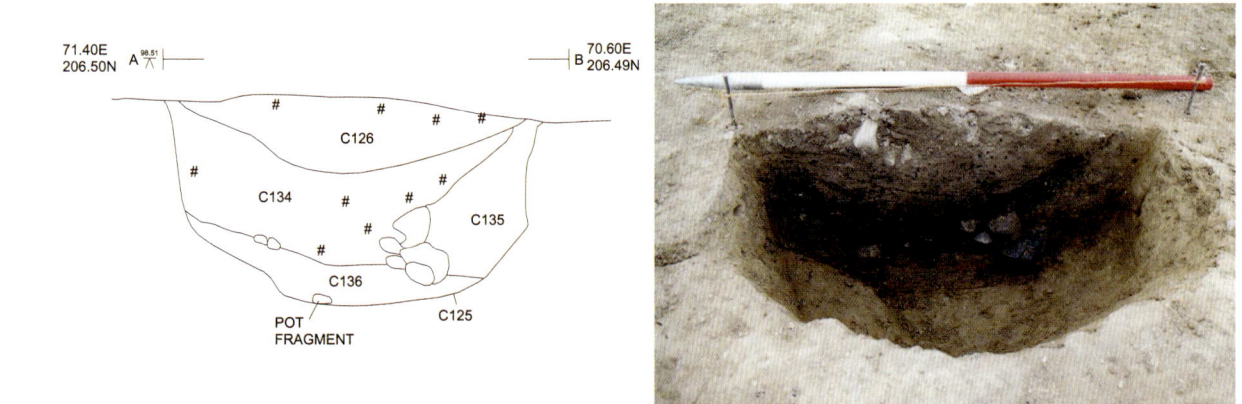

Illus. 9—North-facing section of pit C125 in Area 2 (Valerie J Keeley Ltd).

French Furze and the wider Early Bronze Age world

There is a considerable concentration of prehistoric archaeological remains on the nearby Curragh plains; however, those which have been investigated are predominantly Late Bronze Age or Iron Age in date (Clancy 2006). A sherd of Early Bronze Age bowl tradition pottery was found 9 km away, just south-east of The Curragh plains, at Dún Ailinne (Johnson & Wailes 2007), and bowl tradition burials have been found just over 10 km to the east at Oldtown and Brownstown (Mount et al. 1998) and 11 km to the south-east at Halverstown (Raftery 1940).

The wider distribution of bowl tradition pottery (Illus. 10) shows that it is mainly a northern and eastern Irish phenomenon, with considerable amounts also occurring in western Scotland. However, an increasing number of finds are now coming to light from elsewhere in Ireland (e.g. Jones 1998; Roche & Grogan 2006; Danaher 2004), and it may be that differences in burial practice have obscured the extent of its distribution. For example, a sherd of bowl tradition pottery has been found at

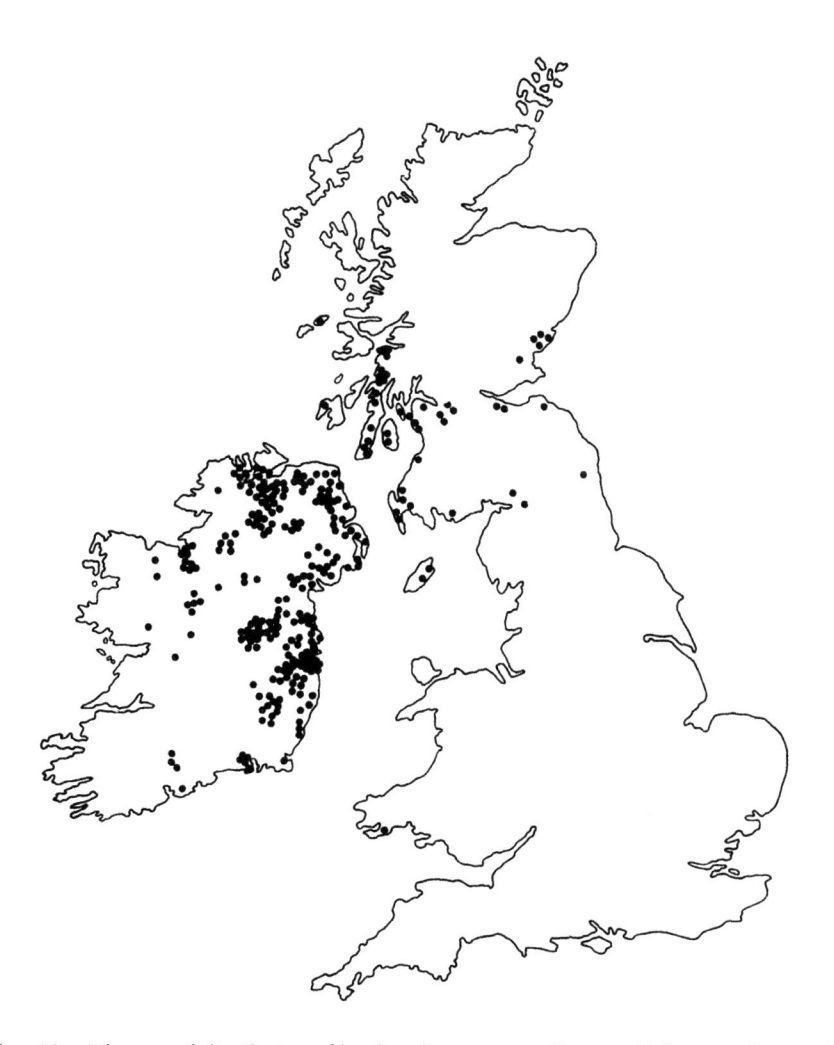

Illus. 10—The general distribution of bowl tradition pottery (from Waddell 2010, fig. 56.1).

Roughan Hill in County Clare (Jones 1998), a site seemingly connected with wedge tombs and among their densest distribution in the country, but where one has yet to be excavated. Nevertheless, the similarities in bowl tradition pottery within the known distribution area attest to closely maintained networks of interaction.

Brindley (2007), through modelling associated radiocarbon dates, was able to propose three chronological stages within Irish bowl tradition pottery. Her study concentrated on material from closed funerary contexts and benefited from the newly available ability to radiocarbon date cremated bone, which is not subject to the 'old wood effect' of oak charcoal. Brindley's chronological stages are distinguishable through the decoration on the pottery, which changes rapidly through time, over large geographical areas. This typo-chronological scheme, if accepted, can provide a tighter date range for ceramic finds than radiocarbon dating alone. (Although Sheridan & Bayliss (2008) have been somewhat critical of Brindley's model, alternative 'formal modelling' (e.g. Bayesian statistics) does not suggest a very different sequence; simply that some of Brindley's groups may start a little earlier and be of slightly shorter duration.) The decoration on the well-preserved French Furze sherd (Illus. 6) is most closely paralleled with that on an unprovenanced tripartite bowl (Ó Ríordáin & Waddell 1993, #244) of Brindley's Stage 3 (A Brindley, pers. comm.) and can thus be tentatively dated to a tighter date range of 1980–1920 BC. This date fits comfortably with the one-sigma (1σ) (68% probability) radiocarbon date range of 2040–1920 BC from French Furze (see Appendix 1).

In contrast to the rather rapid and widespread changing nature of the decoration on the pottery, certain aspects of bowl tradition pots appear to be more regionally restricted and fixed through time. There are, for example, squat tripartite bowls with angular profiles from the north of Ireland (Sheridan 1993, 52 & Fig. 23) and globular ribbed tripartite bowls from Leinster (Sheridan 1993, 57 & Fig. 25), which potters continued to make in those regional forms throughout the decorative changes. With this contrast in mind, it may be possible to gain some insight into Early Bronze Age society through an analogy drawn from an ethnoarchaeological study.

Chaîne opératoire and an ethnoarchaeological study of pottery

The *chaîne opératoire* (French for 'operation chain') approach to studying artefacts was pioneered by palaeontologist Leroi-Gourhan as a method of studying lithics (Audouze 2002). Essentially, it involves viewing an artefact from the perspective of all the stages involved in its production, from raw material to finished product, but further encompassing the understanding that techniques required to complete each stage of a *chaîne opératoire* are social phenomena (Mauss 1934) that involve different degrees of choice (Lemonnier 1993) and require different depths of learning to transmit (Roux & Corbetta 1989).

In an ethnoarchaeological study of traditional African pottery *chaîne opératoire*, Gosselain (1992; 2000) illustrated how, while certain forming techniques involved in making a pot could only be acquired through participation, decoration on the surface of pots was often simply copied. In other words, behind the transmission of these different techniques are different types of interaction that may have a material manifestation apparent in pottery traditions. In the case of our Early Bronze Age bowl tradition pottery, it may be that the more regionally restricted forms are the result of production techniques acquired through participation and therefore most likely to represent intimate networks, such as kin-groups. The geographically more widespread and more rapidly changing decorative elements are likely to represent a less intense type of interaction, perhaps maintained through the exchange of other goods.

Discussion

Although the archaeological remains found at French Furze were of a domestic nature, that does not mean they should be read from a purely functional perspective. We know, from ethnographic studies (Leach 1968), that many societies do not draw as strict a division between the sacred and profane as we sometimes do today (Brück 2006). Ritual life and domestic life are far more likely to have been closely entangled during prehistory (Bradley 2005). The pottery found at French Furze does not appear to have been simply discarded. There are grounds to suggest that it was intentionally deposited as a foundation deposit in the probable entrance of a building and in a pit to the rear of that building. In both cases only a portion of the pot was deposited and in the case of the possible foundation deposit, the sherd may have been retained and handled for some time before deposition. These sherds clearly continued to have significance after the pots to which they belonged were broken. It would be a mistake to consider them as refuse only; we should consider the possible social and ritual roles they and/or their deposition may have played. One possibility is that the pottery, or the material from which it was made, provided a connection with a previous place, person or building; its deposition in the entrance of the house may have invoked that entity to provide some form of spiritual protection. The deposition of the other sherds, in the pit to the rear of the possible structure, may have been necessitated by a fear of spiritual pollution.

It is difficult to know how far personal connections during the Early Bronze Age extended, but the people in Kildare buried their dead with pottery types and in a manner very closely shared with people as far away as Scotland. The widest sphere of interaction was likely maintained and facilitated through the exchange of objects and materials, particularly metals, and may have extended beyond shared pottery traditions. The distribution of bowl tradition pottery suggests, for example, that some of its users may have been pivotal in the exchange of copper between south-western Ireland and the innovative Migdale-Marnoch metal-working area of eastern Scotland (Needham 2004). Direct contacts from one end of such a network to the other were likely infrequent; in most cases, objects and materials probably moved through many intermediaries along a 'down the line' network. However, we should not discount the possibility that some people travelled great distances. Increasing evidence of this is coming to light through isotopic research on human remains (Fitzpatrick 2011), which can demonstrate the geographic regions from which people originated. At a broad regional scale there were elements of a shared ideology expressed through the use of similar pottery, especially in burials, across which decorative fashions spread relatively quickly. Then, at a more local scale again, in the regionally restricted pottery forms, it may be possible to identify closer spheres of interaction, perhaps representing kin groups.

Conclusions

Accounts of the Early Bronze Age, and of prehistory more generally, are often dominated by the funerary record. The manner in which communities buried their dead can reflect a lot about their shared beliefs and about how they organised their societies. Burial rituals can take an idealised form, however, and may actually furnish limited information about how people lived their lives in practice. The significance of a site like French Furze lies in how it allows us to examine the daily practices, such as the use and deposition of pottery, through which Early Bronze Age communities actively engaged with, and negotiated their place in, their world. Examining the *chaîne opératoire* of techniques behind the production of pottery allows us to move beyond the distribution of 'pottery traditions' and can reveal more nuanced aspects of the spheres of interaction in which those communities were involved.

Acknowledgements

I would like to express my appreciation to all the staff who worked on site at French Furze and to all the specialists who contributed to subsequent analysis. Special thanks are due to Dr Anna Brindley, who gave very generously of her time to correspond with me on my various questions, and to Dr Charles Mount for information on his ongoing research. I would also like to thank Valerie J Keeley for employing me to direct the excavation, my Ph.D supervisor Dr Carleton Jones for his continued support, my father Pat Muldoon for reading and commenting on an early draft, the NRA for inviting me to speak and the editors for offering comments on this paper. Finally, I would also like to thank Yolande O'Brien, a fellow Ph.D student at NUI Galway, for scanning and sending me an article so I could complete this paper.

4. Castlefarm 1 and the working of skeletal materials in early medieval rural Ireland

Ian Riddler & Nicola Trzaska-Nartowski

The working of skeletal materials in early medieval rural Ireland (c. AD 500–900) has attracted attention in recent years as attempts are made to synthesise a wealth of data from pre-development archaeological excavations conducted in the last decade or more. The craft has been discussed in two recent reports on crafts and the economy of early medieval rural settlements, including some of those excavated as part of NRA road schemes (Comber 2008; Seaver 2012). Both authors have approached the craft by first considering the actual objects made from skeletal materials and take the view that antler-, bone- and horn-working were neither highly specialised nor necessarily a full-time occupation. The craft was not a specialist undertaking because it was not a full-time occupation and it was thought to require only a rudimentary level of ability. An exception lies with comb-making, which, it is conceded, may have been a specialist undertaking (Comber 2008, 97; Seaver 2012, 63).

The finished objects have gained much more attention than the waste material produced during their manufacture, yet if the waste is placed at the forefront and examined across the working sequence, it can provide significant details about the

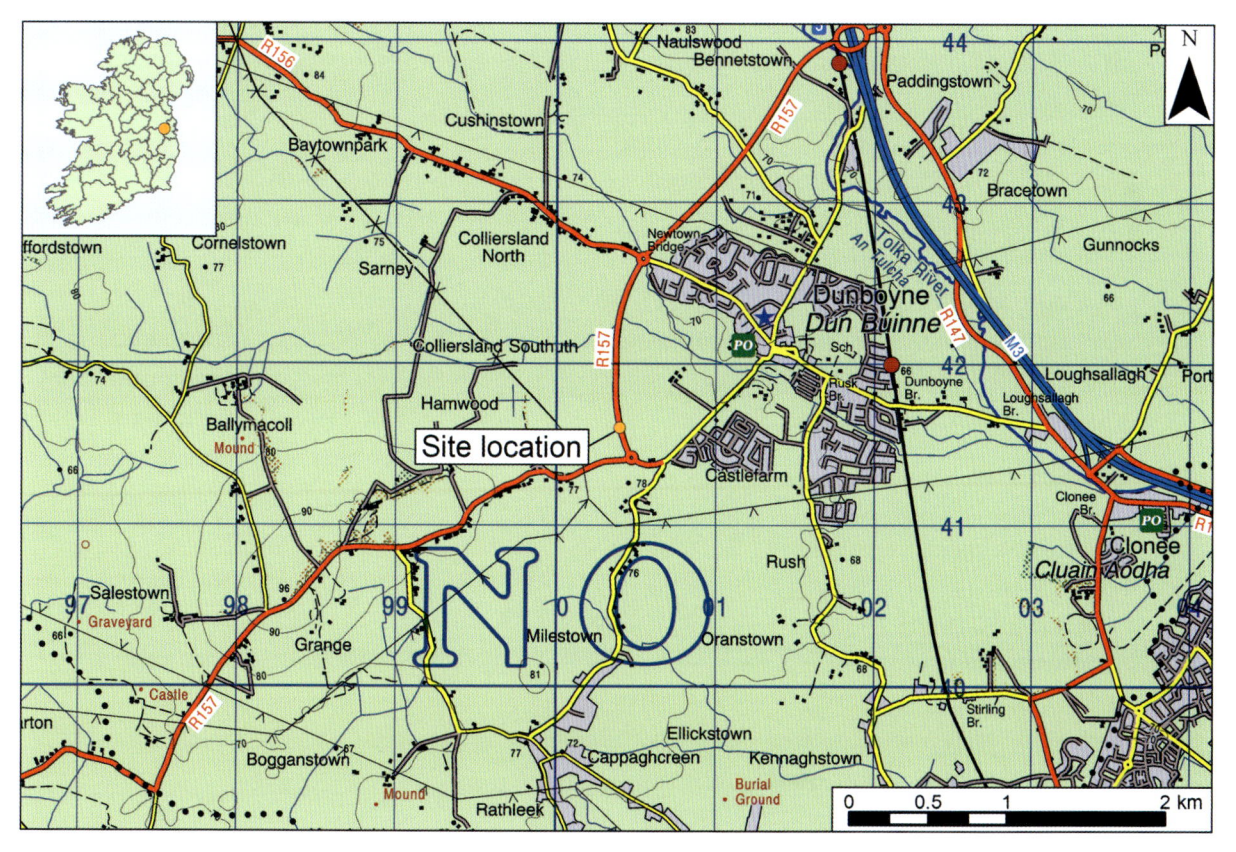

Illus. 1—Location of Castlefarm 1, Co. Meath (based on the Ordnance Survey Ireland Discovery Series map).

choice of raw materials, the location of the craft, the tools and processes of object manufacture and the scale of production. With that in mind, it is appropriate to reappraise the evidence for the craft, with an emphasis placed firmly on the waste materials. The focus here lies with antler and bone waste from a single site: an enclosed settlement at Castlefarm 1, Co. Meath (Illus. 1), which was excavated in advance of the construction of the M3 motorway (O'Connell 2009; O'Connell & Clark 2009).[1] Although horn-working should not be forgotten, there is insufficient evidence, as yet, to review its role within this craft framework.

Antler-working at Castlefarm

Antler waste has not been found on every early medieval rural site in Ireland and in general the quantities recovered are small. A range of excavated sites are shown in Illus. 2, each of which has produced at least five antler offcuts. Of these 20 sites, only five have yielded more than 20 offcuts, and nine sites produced less than 10 offcuts. Two sites stand out from the remainder. More than 400 antler fragments were found during excavations within the New Graveyard at Clonmacnoise, Co. Offaly. Over 40% of this assemblage comprised debris from a workshop and provided important evidence for comb-making on site (King 1996, 77; 2009, 339; Seaver 2012, 62). The other significant settlement is Castlefarm 1, which produced 128 offcuts of antler.

The antler waste from Castlefarm was derived from the fills of enclosure ditches, pits, wells and post-holes. It was concentrated in a small number of features, however: 74% of the waste came from contexts related to the inner enclosure ditch, and almost 10% was recovered from the outer enclosure ditch and its extension (Illus. 3). Outside of the enclosure ditches antler waste was sparsely dispersed, with less than five offcuts coming from most of the fills of the pits or wells, the majority of which were close to the enclosure ditches.

A similar pattern in the deposition of antler waste can be seen across contemporary sites. Enclosure ditches were the preferred locations for the disposal of such waste across most of the sites in Illus. 2, although other ditch-like features were also used. Thus at both Ballynacarriga 2, Co. Cork, and Mackney, Co. Galway, antler waste was found in the fills of souterrains (underground structures used for refuge and/ or storage), while at Killoteran 9, Co. Waterford, it was recovered from the wheel-pit and tail-race of a watermill. In contrast to contemporary urban sites in northern Europe, antler waste was not deposited close to habitation structures, but was carried some distance away to the enclosure ditches, which formed significant edges to the settlement (O'Sullivan & Nicholl 2011, 86–7). This means, of course, that unless substantial parts of the enclosure ditches are excavated, antler waste may not be recovered from a rural settlement, particularly when the waste usually occurs only at certain locations within the ditch fills. Moreover, simply quantifying the amount

---

[1] NGR 300394, 241605; height 73 m OD; Excavation Reg. No. E3023; Ministerial Direction No. A017; Excavation Director Aidan O'Connell.

of antler waste recovered is not an accurate way of assessing the level of production using skeletal materials within a settlement; the waste needs to be examined more closely to determine the quantity of antlers worked and the production stages present. A small amount of waste can sometimes reflect large production circumstances and vice versa.

The deposition of antler waste at Castlefarm occurred largely within the early medieval sub-phases of occupation, which produced 84% of the material. Phase IIa extended between the early fifth and mid-seventh century and Phase IIb between

Table 1—Antler waste from the inner enclosure ditch at Castlefarm, by production stage and sub-phase.

Feature	Context	Production stage 1	2	3	4	Total per sub-phase
Sub–phase IIa							
36	58		2			4
	202		1			
	212		1			
96	539	1				7
	454		3			
	323			2		
	452			1		
Sub–phase IIb							
36	34	1	2	5		13
	201	1	1	1	2	
96	486	4	3	4	2	14
	322		1			
Sub–phase IIc							
36	199	5	3	6		14
96	224	5	2	2		26
	309	1	2	6		
	581	1	1			
	311		3			
	575		1	1		
	674			1		

Fragments of Lives Past

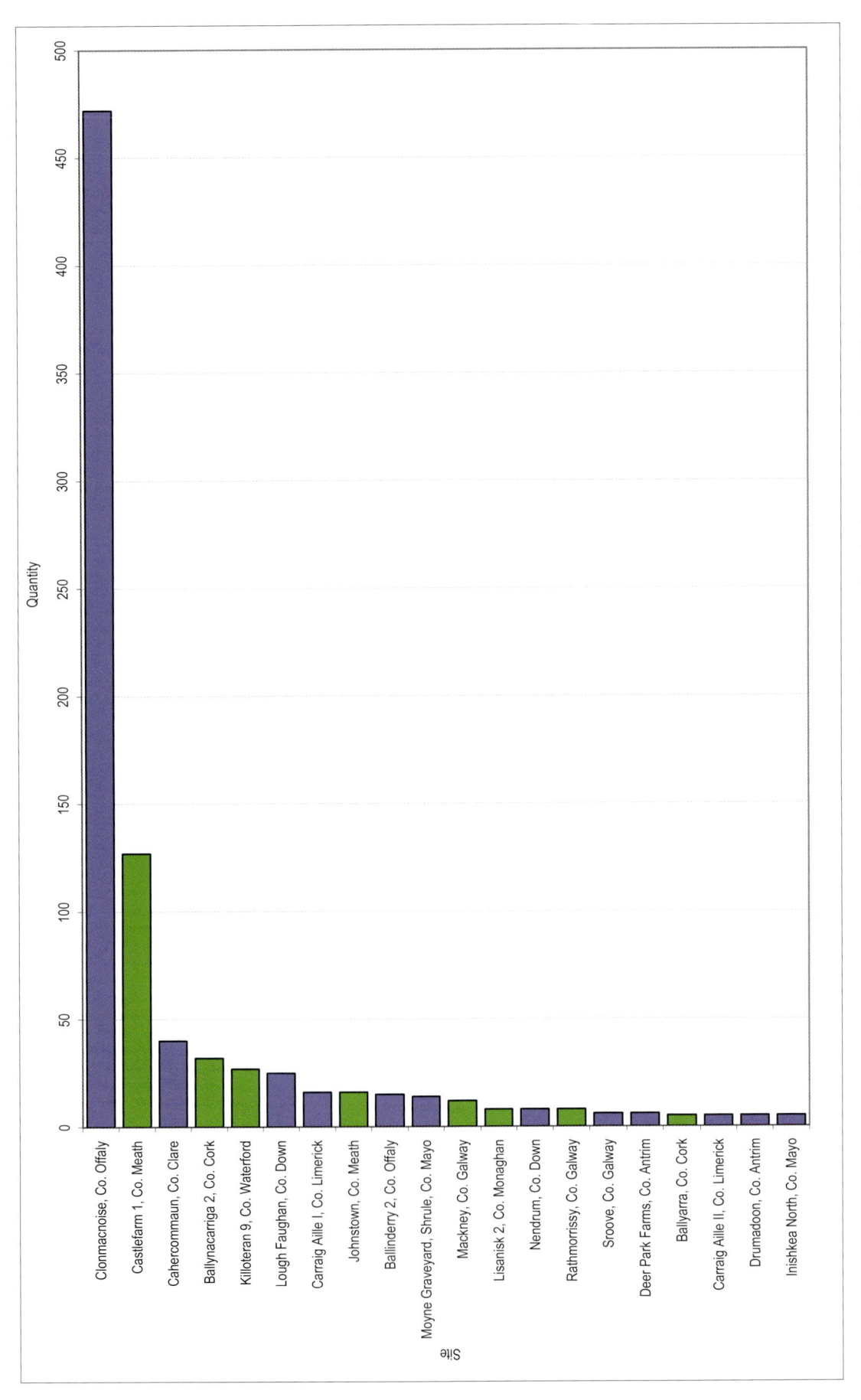

Illus. 2—*Quantity of antler waste recovered from Irish early medieval rural settlements, with sites from national roads shown in green (Ian Riddler & Nicola Trzaska-Nartowski).*

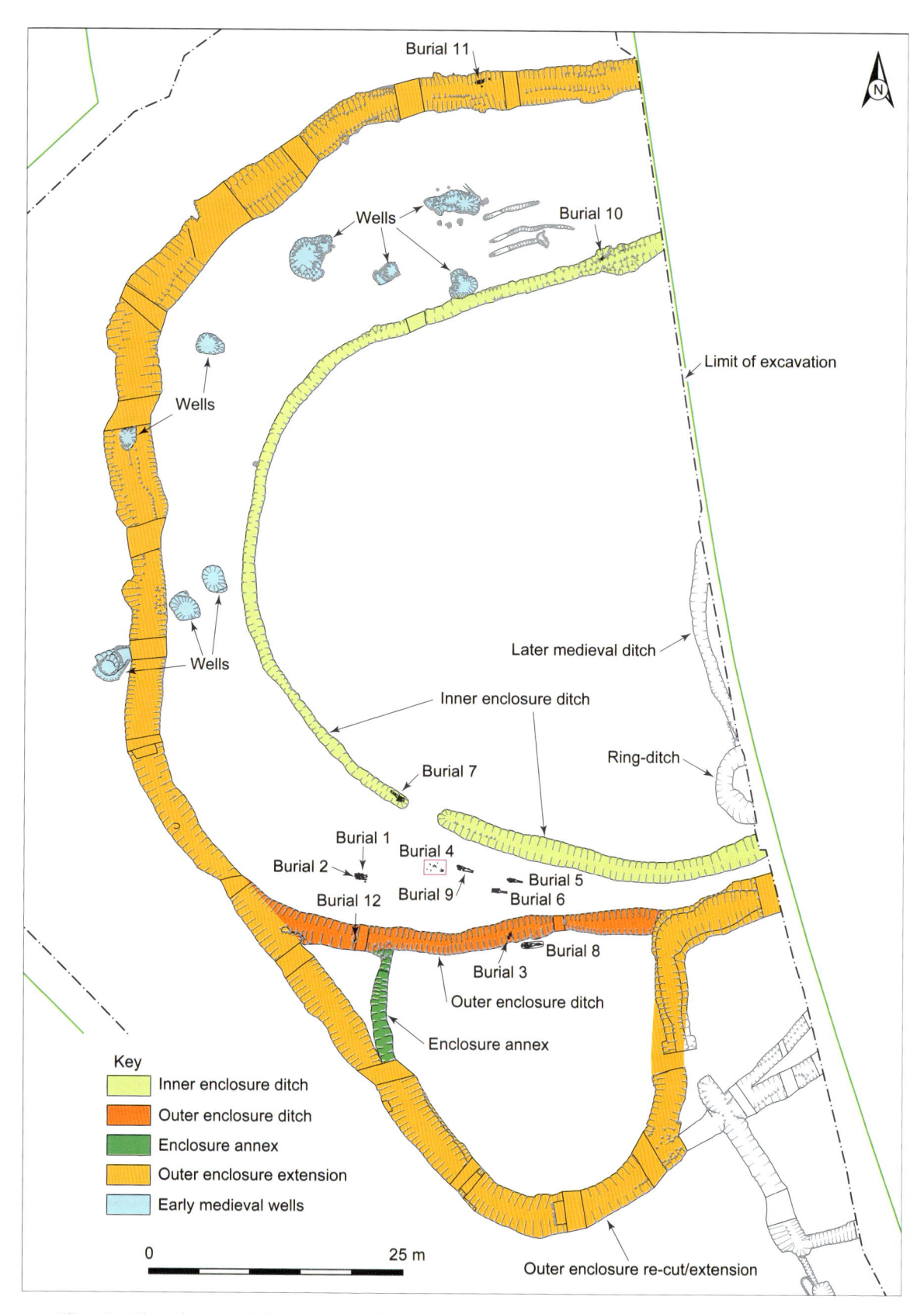

Illus. 3—Plan of excavated features at Castlefarm 1, Co. Meath (Archaeological Consultancy Services Ltd).

the early seventh and the early ninth century, with Phase IIc largely overlapping with the previous phase and dated from between the mid-seventh and the early ninth century (O'Connell & Clark 2009). Within each of these sub-phases, small quantities of antler were discarded into the northern (F96) and southern (F36) parts of the inner enclosure ditch (Table 1); around half of this ditch lay beyond the limit of excavation (O'Connell 2009, illus. 3.4). The total amount of antler waste per sub-phase is not large, but it increases over time, from 11 fragments in Phase IIa to 27 fragments in Phase IIb and 40 fragments in Phase IIc. The scale of production may have been increasing from the sixth to the eighth century, although each manufacturing episode would still have been small.

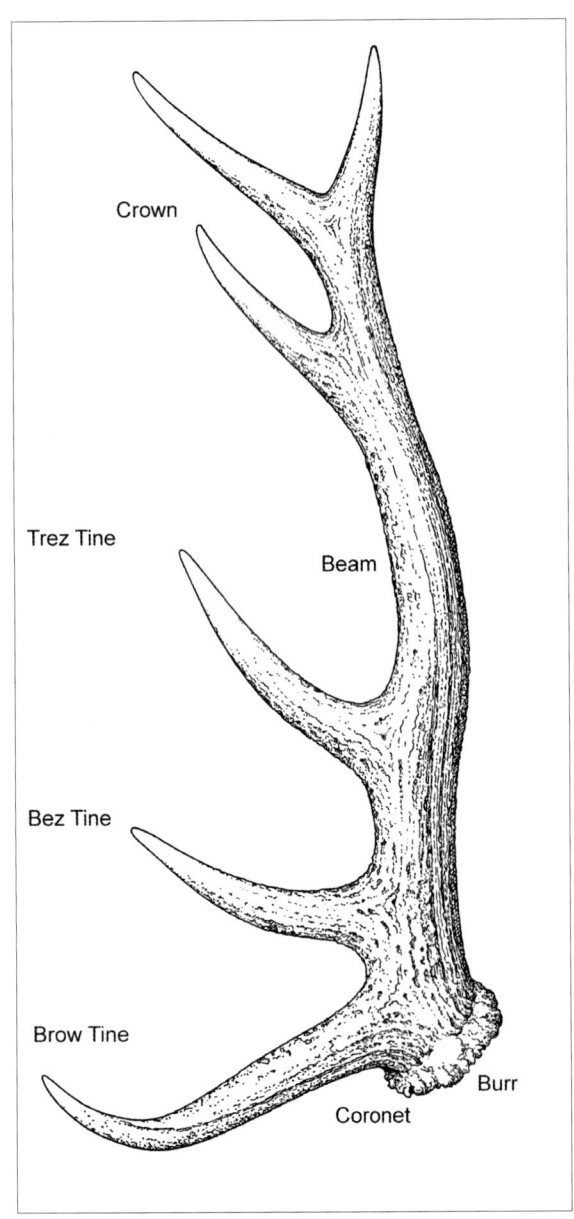

Illus. 4—The terminology of antler (after Ulbricht 1978, fig. 3).

The antler waste provides abundant clues about the stages of production, of which there are four, and the tools used by the craftworker. The stages consist of initial dismemberment, secondary reduction of the material into segments, followed by shaping the material to form the object components and, finally, assembling and finishing the objects. In the first stage the burr, crown and tines are separated from the beam (see Illus. 4), so that the antler itself is effectively reduced to its component parts. Twenty-four crown offcuts from Castlefarm belong to this stage, alongside five near-complete tines and six burrs, together weighing just over 5 kg. Most of the antler was separated by sawing, either cleanly in a single direction across a surface or by sawing from several directions and snapping away the spongy tissue (known as cortile or trabecular tissue) at the centre of the antler. In some cases tines had been hacked away from the antler with the use of a knife or a small axe. This working method, which is much more onerous than sawing, is found largely in Phase IIc.

Sawing of the antler was not always completely successful. Fifteen saw marks were recorded, each representing an initial attempt to saw into the antler, which was then abandoned. These marks were measured to provide an indication of the widths of the saw blades used. They range from 1.2 mm to 3.2 mm in width and correspond well with the values obtained from the antler from Clonmacnoise. In contrast, 12th-century antler waste from excavations on High Street in Dublin City was dismembered with thinner saw blades (Illus. 5). Thinner saw blades came into use in Ireland during the 12th century, when the processing of antler became more intricate, reflecting the finer and more delicate combs being produced in the country at that time (Riddler & Trzaska-Nartowski, forthcoming). The evidence from the three sites indicates that an antler worker possessed at least two saws, one of which was used for finer, more precise sawing, and by the 12th century this interest in fine, precise cutting had extended also to the initial stages of antler working.

From the earliest stage in the process, the waste itself indicates that the antler worker was thinking about the final product; it may have been as simple as an antler pick or as complex as the composite comb. Seven antler picks were identified at Castlefarm, five of which came from the fills of the inner enclosure ditch. They occur in three different types. The first type retains the burr and part of the beam, and uses the brow tine as the blade. The second type uses either the bez or the trez tine as the blade and both the burr and the brow tine are removed. The third type consists of the brow tine and adjacent section of beam, which is hollowed to allow a wooden

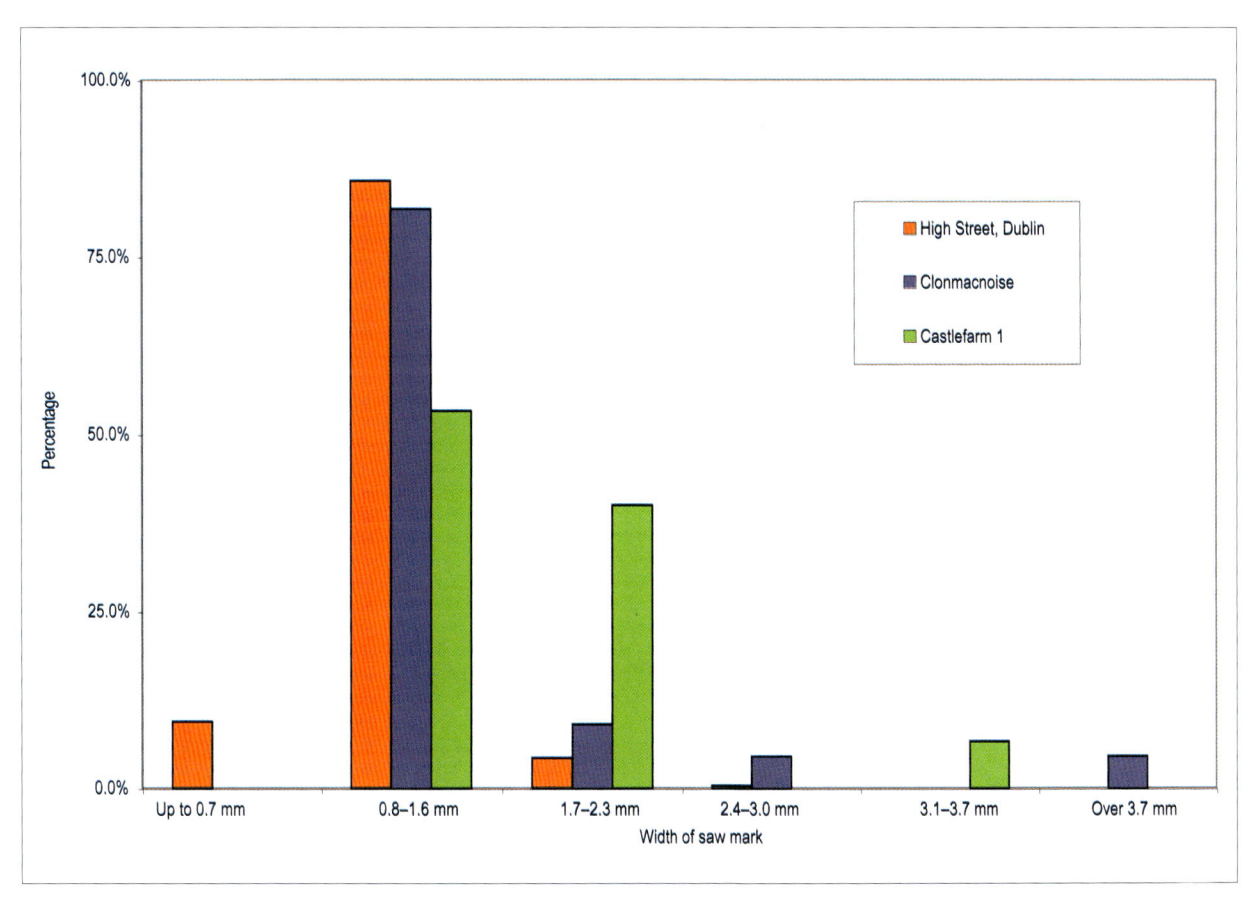

Illus. 5—Widths of saw marks on worked antler from Castlefarm 1, Clonmacnoise and High Street, Dublin (Ian Riddler & Nicola Trzaska-Nartowski).

shaft to be secured to it. Small antlers from young deer were used, possibly because these required little modification in order to be used as picks (Illus. 6). The larger antlers were retained for complete dismemberment and working into other objects. This selection process is effectively the reverse of the situation in Bronze Age Ireland, where the largest antlers were used as picks.

During the second stage of production the beam and tines were sawn into smaller segments. The burrs could be prepared for lathe-turning at this point, in order to be made into spindle whorls, but at Castlefarm a number were simply discarded. Most of the ends of the tines were also sawn away, while the straighter sections, located closer to the beam, were retained as the raw material for use as handles for a range of small implements. Handles were produced from straight or lightly curved sections of antler tines, which were smoothed across the outer surface and hollowed, removing the cortile tissue at the centre. Evidence for their manufacture has been found at Cathedral Hill, Co. Armagh, as well as at Castlefarm, while the handles themselves are common finds on early medieval sites in Ireland. The waste discarded at this stage is smaller in size (26 offcuts) and lighter in weight (just over 2.1 kg).

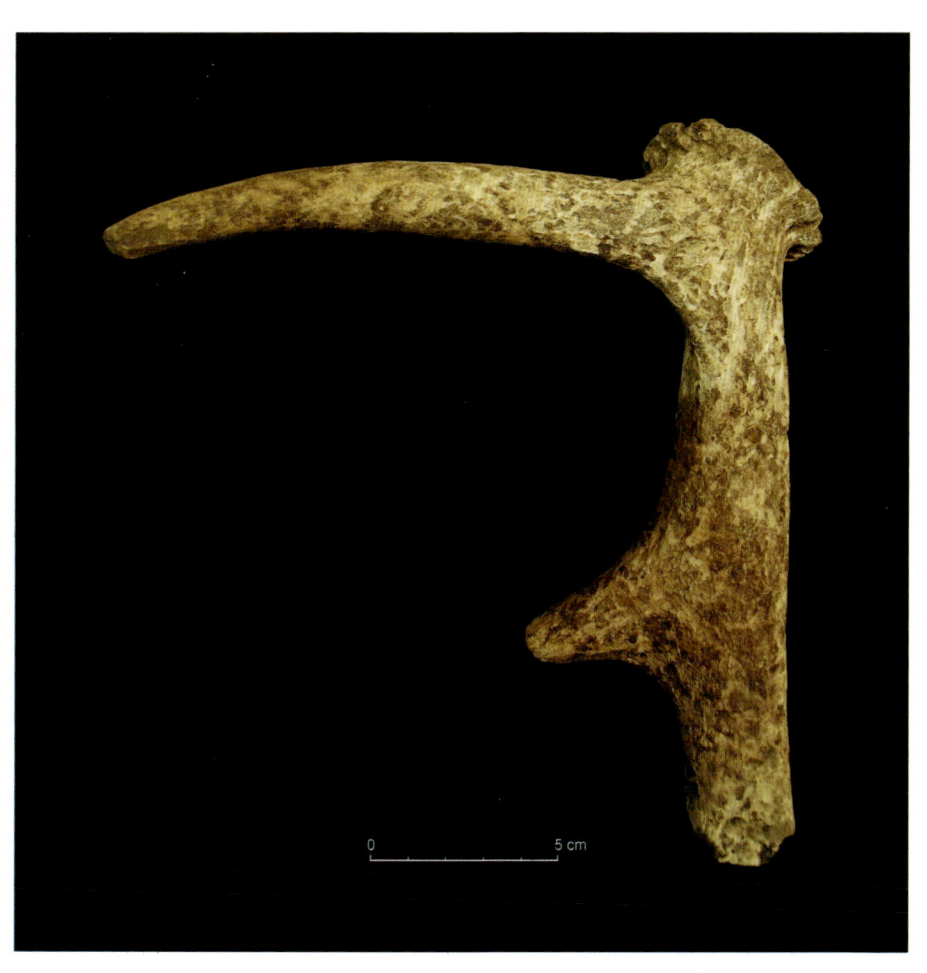

Illus. 6—An antler pick from Castlefarm 1 (Ian Riddler & Nicola Trzaska-Nartowski).

Illus. 7—Antler combs from Castlefarm 1 (Ian Riddler & Nicola Trzaska-Nartowski).

Aside from picks and handles, the other object type for which there is good production evidence from Castlefarm is the composite comb. The majority of combs of this period consisted of tooth and end segments, which were fastened to connecting plates with iron or antler rivets, with sets of teeth cut on one or both sides of the connecting plates (Illus. 7). The various processes of comb manufacture can be traced within the antler waste. As mentioned above, the beam was sawn into segments during the second stage of antler-processing, which inevitably provided some awkward pieces at the junctions with the tines (Illus. 8). Twenty-nine examples of these beam/tine junctions were recovered. They were thrown away by the antler workers, but only after any useful section of antler had been removed from them (the third stage). The cutting and trimming of the antler during this stage reduced it to longer lengths suitable for the connecting plates of the combs, and shorter segments, which were to become the tooth segments. An unfinished tooth segment was recovered from the topsoil overlying the site (Illus. 9), alongside several small fragments derived from the trimming of these segments to shape. Antler shavings, which reflect the paring of objects to shape with a knife or drawknife (a knife with the handle set perpendicular to the blade), also provide good evidence for working at the third stage. These were not found or did not survive at Castlefarm, but several have come from Raystown, Co. Meath (Illus. 10), another extensive enclosed settlement,

Illus. 8—The junction of a beam and tine from a red deer antler from Castlefarm 1 (Ian Riddler & Nicola Trzaska-Nartowski).

Illus. 9—An unfinished antler tooth segment from a composite comb from Castlefarm 1 (Ian Riddler & Nicola Trzaska-Nartowski).

c. 11 km to the north-east. Forty-four offcuts from Castlefarm can be identified for this stage, weighing 1.8 kg. Thus the first three stages of antler-working at Castlefarm are roughly even in terms of the quantity of offcuts that can be assigned to them, but the offcuts are increasingly reduced in size and weight as the antler is cut and trimmed to shape.

Judging from the waste material alone, the antler worker(s) used at least two saws, as well as a variety of other implements, including knives, drawknives and a small lathe. The use of other tools, including drills, files and abrasives, can be established from examining perforations and worked surfaces on the objects. Hone stones to sharpen these tools would also have formed an important part of the antler worker's tool-kit, who would have manufactured his own tools. These included antler wedges—essentially tine ends that taper to pointed terminals and could be used to split sections of antler. Three antler wedges were found at Castlefarm, one of which came from a Phase IIc context, while a second example was later in date and the third wedge derived from the topsoil (Illus. 11).

Illus. 10—Antler shavings from Raystown, Co. Meath (courtesy of Matthew Seaver).

Illus. 11—Antler wedges from Castlefarm 1 (Ian Riddler & Nicola Trzaska-Nartowski).

Bone-working at Castlefarm

One of the surprising elements of the Castlefarm assemblage is the presence of 48 pig fibulae, some of which had been made into needles and awls, while others are unfinished objects. (The fibula is the outer and narrower hind-leg bone.) It is very unusual to find any unfinished pig fibulae objects on early medieval sites. Here the production stages in their manufacture can be traced, much as for the antler waste. The assemblage includes seven entirely unmodified fibulae. Five examples had been partially modified, either by trimming the upper or lower end of the bone, or by preparing a tapering shaft; in one case, an attempt to perforate the head can be seen (Illus. 12). The finished objects include 18 needles and nine objects that can be described as awls. These closely resemble the needles but have no perforations through the head. Their functional interpretation is drawn from texts dealing with objects from later prehistory, where they are customarily grouped with a variety of other bone objects also regarded as awls (Seager Smith 2000, 224, fig 89). They form very useful objects that fit well in the hand, although the points can be a little fragile. They have previously been regarded as pins, but Continental research, in particular, has indicated that they are not dress accessories (Westphalen 1999, 15, plate 4.12–14). It is possible that they were used on looms, as textile manufacturing implements, although they may have had a variety of functions.

Illus. 12—Unfinished, worked pig fibulae from Castlefarm 1. Attempted perforation of one example shown at A (Ian Riddler & Nicola Trzaska-Nartowski).

The distribution of the pig fibulae is remarkably similar to that of the antler waste in terms both of their location and the quantities deposited over time, with 29 examples associated with the fills of the inner enclosure ditch across the three sub-phases and nine coming from the outer enclosure ditch or its extension. The remaining 10 were found in the fills of nearby pits and wells. There seems little doubt that the antler-worker was also the bone-worker and that relatively simple object types, made from readily accessible animal remains, lay firmly within the domain of a specialist. It could be suggested that antler- and bone-working was undertaken by separate individuals who disposed of their waste in exactly the same places, at the same time, so that the waste can then be regarded more as the product of a workshop than a single individual. But studies of worked skeletal materials from London, in particular, have also established that antler, bone and horn were worked there at the same time and used interchangeably to manufacture the same products, with combs, pins and needles all made of both bone and antler (Riddler & Trzaska-Nartowski 2012; Keily et al. 2012). It is difficult not to believe that the same situation prevailed at Castlefarm 1 and that antler, bone and horn were all worked by the same person—rather than postulating an arbitrary division of workload by material.

Conclusion

The scale of antler- and bone-working at Castlefarm was always small, with each production episode using just a few antlers. From a single antler it is possible to produce three to four combs, a spindle whorl and several implement handles. Experimental work (Ambrosiani 1981, 103–18) indicates that composite combs like those found at Castlefarm 1 (Illus. 7) take two to three days to manufacture, while handles and spindle whorls would take just a few hours each. With bone-working added to the equation, an episode of antler- and bone-working may have lasted for several weeks, or even longer, based on these estimates of the time taken to manufacture each object type. The range of antler objects found at the site extends beyond combs, handles and spindle whorls to notched tine implements, gaming pieces, pins and mounts, whilst cattle and sheep bone were used for spearheads and pin-beaters, as well as pins, needles and awls.

The small quantities of antler waste from individual contexts at Castlefarm reflect the seasonal nature of the craft, which probably took place in the spring and early summer, using both antler and bone. The antlers of male red deer are shed in the spring and the craft may have begun each year when this raw material became available. As such, the craft was not a full-time occupation, but neither were other crafts in early medieval Ireland. The archaeological evidence for textile-working, for example, is scant and difficult to correlate with the sparse historical sources; but the absence of artefacts should not be used to suggest that these were highly specialist activities, carried out at just a small number of places (Comber 2008, 99–110). In later peasant communities some elements of weaving were carried out communally, not in specialist workshops, but simply as groups of women working together at certain times of the year (Walton Rogers 2007, 46). Life was seasonal, with crop cultivation, hunting and fishing all occupying different parts of the year. Weaving was also a seasonal craft, being dependent on the shearing of sheep in the summer and the growing of flax and hemp, harvested in the autumn. Women may have spent a lot of their waking hours engaged in the various elements of the weaving process, but that does not mean that it was a full-time occupation (ibid., 9–10). Antler- and bone-working in early medieval rural Ireland was a craft of seasonal production episodes, each of a relatively small scale, producing objects for local use. Other crafts, including metal-working and textile manufacture, depended on tools produced by the antler- and bone-worker. The worker of skeletal materials used antler, bone and horn for the manufacture of a wide range of implements. It is significant that even the simplest of these items, like bone needles, were produced by a craftsman who, on that basis, can be regarded as a specialist.

Acknowledgements

We are very grateful to Mary Deevy, Maria Lear, Donald Murphy and Matt Seaver for enabling us to examine and record objects and waste of antler and bone from recent excavations.

5. An early medieval copper-alloy ladle from Ballynapark, Co. Wicklow

Noel Dunne

The field opposite Jack White's public house on the N11 in County Wicklow yielded an unexpected, isolated, but intriguing find in the form of an early medieval copper-alloy ladle (Illus. 1–3). Here, in Ballynapark townland, 10 km north of Arklow, the ground is low-lying, flat and marshy, with a deep organic soil resting on white marl. Prior to reclamation, this ground would have been bogland. The surrounding terrain consists of a crescent-shaped, undulating coastal plain sandwiched between the foothills of the Wicklow Mountains and the Irish Sea and stretching from Bray to Arklow. The linear expanse of Brittas Bay is only 3 km to the east. Investigations at Ballynapark for the N11 Rathnew–Arklow road scheme in 2006, supervised by Excavation Director Goorik Dehaene for Irish Archaeological Consultancy Ltd, revealed a number of ploughed-out *fulachtaí fia* (burnt mounds) dating from the Middle Neolithic period (c. 3600–2900 BC) to the Early Bronze Age (c. 2200–1600 BC).[1] The remains comprised a concentration of pits, troughs, post-holes and a stone platform; all overlaid by spreads of burnt stone (Dehaene 2009). These prehistoric features provided no indication of the surprise find, from a much later period, that was to be discovered.

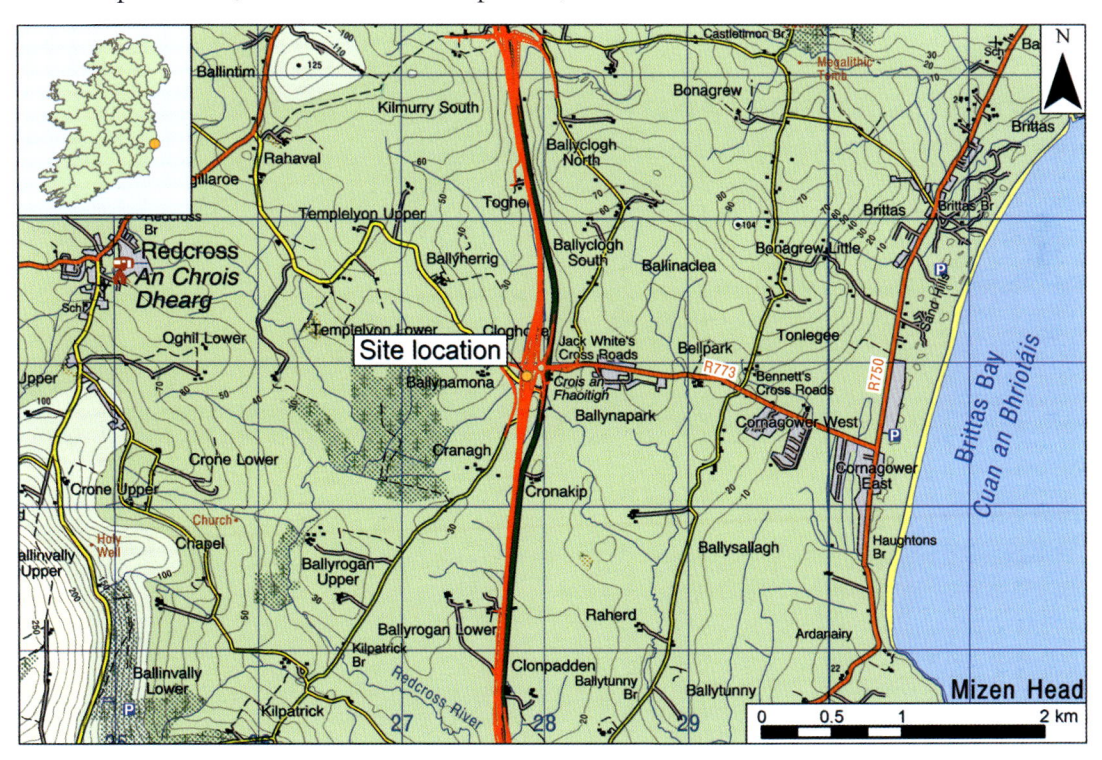

Illus. 1—Location of Ballynapark, Co. Wicklow (based on the Ordnance Survey Ireland Discovery Series map).

---

[1] NGR 327882, 182909; height 26 m OD; Excavation Reg. No. E3220; Ministerial Direction No. A022; Excavation Director Goorik Dehaene.

Fragments of Lives Past

Illus. 2—The well-preserved handle and disc-shaped terminal of the Ballynapark ladle, following conservation by the National Museum of Ireland (John Sunderland).

An early medieval copper-alloy ladle from Ballynapark, Co. Wicklow

Illus. 3—The front and back of the ladle (John Sunderland).

The Ballynapark ladle

The copper-alloy ladle (Find No. E3220/A022/035:01:006) was recovered from the interface of the organic soil and the underlying marl in the course of mechanically stripping topsoil overlying the archaeological features, prior to their full excavation by hand. The find-spot was close to, but distinct from, one of the spreads of burnt stone. The handle and its disc-shaped terminal are well preserved (Illus. 2), but only a portion of the ladle's rounded bowl and rim survives. No modern fractures are apparent, hence the object was either in a damaged condition when originally deposited, or else the thinner bowl and rim have suffered differential deterioration since deposition (Illus. 3 & 4).

The estimated original dimensions of the ladle are 385 mm for the overall length and 114 mm for the outer diameter of the bowl. The handle is 10 mm wide by 6–8 mm thick and the disc terminal has a diameter of 46 mm. The handle is flanged along both sides, creating a H-shaped cross-section, which would have contributed significantly to its strength. What was initially thought to be soil imbedded along its front and back lengths proved to be wood inlays between the flanges, which were identified during conservation treatment (Illus. 5). The inlays were extremely deteriorated and are now mainly a mixture of soil and wood fibres, so that less than a third of the wood structure is preserved (Koehler 2009).

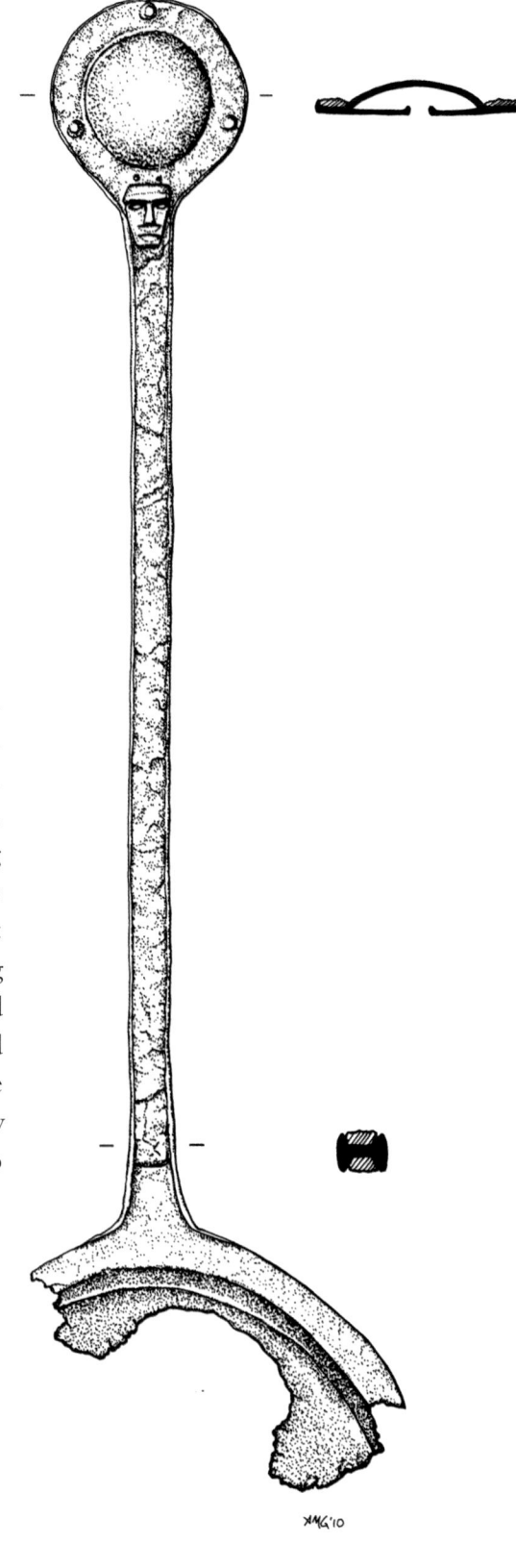

Illus. 4—A post-conservation drawing of the Ballynapark ladle (Alva Mac Gowan, Irish Archaeological Consultancy Ltd).

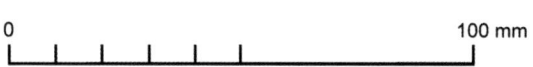

Illus. 5—Close-up of the ladle handle showing the wood inlay between the flanges (John Sunderland).

The front of the disc-shaped handle terminal has a central domed boss in tinned bronze that would have made it look like silver (a common treatment in early medieval metalwork). Some of the tinning is in a very good condition. A band around the circumference incorporates deteriorated organic matter, likely to be further wood inlay. Three rivets within this band functioned to hold a convex back-plate in position, which is also of tinned bronze. This rounded back-plate displays a central perforation, which would have held a hanging ring that unfortunately no longer survives.

The surviving portion of the bowl indicates that it was of thin sheet metal, about 1 mm thick, and had a squat, hemispherical form. A rounded ridge around the circumference, immediately below the rim, would have added strength to the bowl. The only evidence of bowl decoration consists of a single incised line around the circumference, along the shoulder between the rim and the bowl. This line could also have acted as a guide in the manufacture of the bowl. The handle flanges taper to the flat rim. On the underside of the rim, at the junction with the handle, the surface of the metal is lightly scored with short regular lines, probably formed with a chisel. These are likely to represent an overrun of the keying for the glue that would have held the wood inlays securely in place; such glue may have been beeswax.

A stylised bronze human head is positioned on the front of the ladle, at the end of the handle, before the disc terminal (Illus. 6). This head faces down the handle and is wedge-shaped, with prominent features in a chiselled, wood-cut style. Bulging oval eyes are set under a heavy overhanging brow. A prominent ridge forms a wedge-shaped nose, while deep chiselled grooves define the upper lip and mouth. A line above the brow probably indicates some form of headgear. The head has a flat top, with two holes immediately above perforating the handle, extending through the back-plate of the terminal. These holes would have facilitated rivets that anchored some form of mount or crown above the head. At the opposite end of the handle, at the junction with the bowl, the original presence of an opposing second head that faced up the handle is indicated by a 'ghost shadow' and some lead solder (Illus. 7). There is no corresponding pair of holes perforating the handle at this location, perhaps indicating that there was no corresponding crown or mount with this head.

The wood inlays may have consisted of a polished hardwood, such as yew, which would have added considerably to the overall colour and aesthetics of the ladle. It is also tempting to envisage the surface of the wood being painted and possibly bearing decoration linking both human heads.

Illus. 6—The stylised bronze human head on the front of the ladle, at the end of the handle, before the disc terminal (John Sunderland).

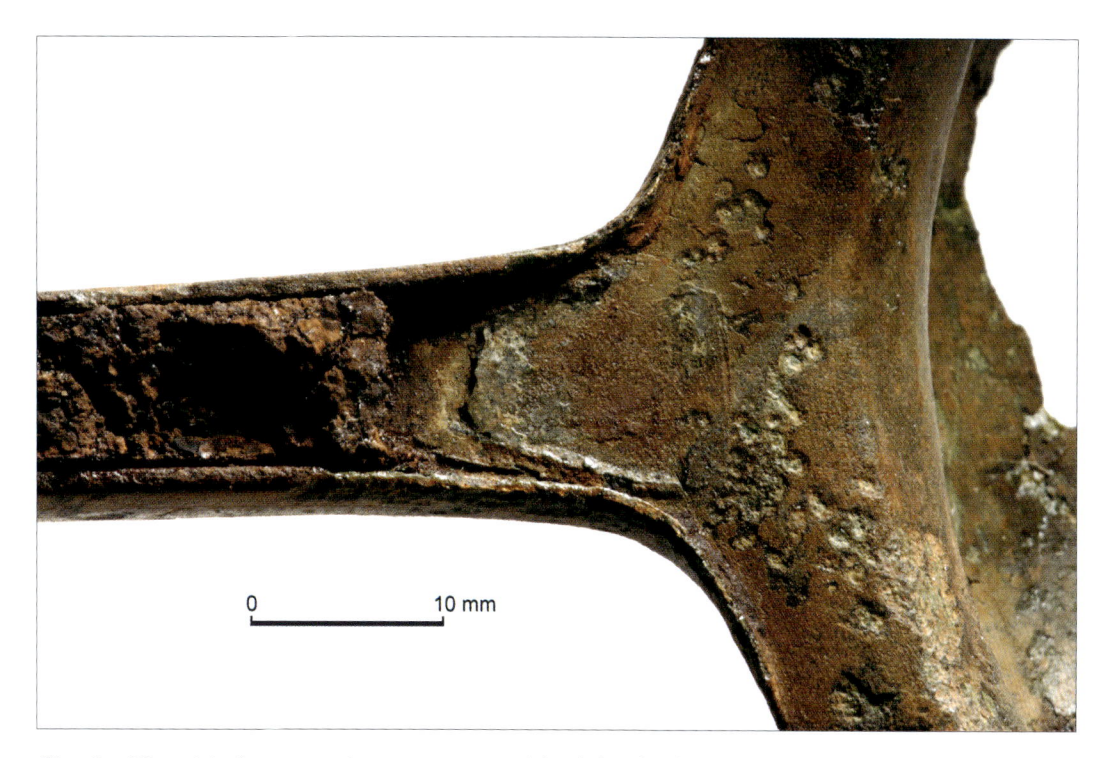

Illus. 7—The original presence of an opposing second head that faced up the handle is indicated by a 'ghost shadow' and some lead solder at the opposite end of the handle, at the junction with the bowl (John Sunderland).

Artistic and functional parallels

Opposing heads or matching faces in mirror-image are recurring elements of early medieval manuscript illumination and metalwork in Ireland, very elegantly demonstrated by the opposing heads that link the terminals on the Cavan Brooch (Illus. 8). This is a cast, gilt silver brooch, dating from the late eighth to early ninth century AD, with each of the two expanded terminals and the head of the pin grasped by the biting jaws of three animal heads (Wallace & Ó Floinn 2002, 184, 202). Comparisons for the Ballynapark head can be made with an anthropomorphic mount, originally from an Irish hanging-bowl, discovered near the coast at Arnside, Cumbria, in north-west England (Youngs & Herepath 2001). This copper-alloy mount, dating from the eighth century, incorporates a stylised human face set above a square panel of geometric sunken cells that were originally filled with brightly coloured enamel—a process known as *champlevé* enamelling, where cells are either carved, etched, die struck or cast in metal and filled with vitreous enamel (Illus. 9). The Cumbrian mount is likely to have been Viking loot or treasure and had been cut-down or refashioned. It was originally symmetrical, with a matching face in mirror-image set on the opposite side of the enamelled panel, and would have formed one of a set of three rim-mounts for a hanging-bowl of thin copper-alloy sheeting. The function of these mounts was to anchor the rings and chains by which the bowl was hung. The human face has

Illus. 8—The Cavan Brooch, dating from the late eighth to early ninth century AD, with a close-up of the mirrored heads (these images are reproduced with the kind permission of the National Museum of Ireland).

been described as 'grim' and 'staring' (ibid.) and bears considerable similarities to the Ballynapark head, with large bulging eyes and a prominent ridge forming a wedge-shaped nose. The top of the head is also flat and this may have facilitated the rim of the hanging-bowl. The cheeks are high, with the mouth defined by a down-turned segment above a prominent chin. Unlike the Ballynapark head, prominent ears are present.

Comparisons can also be made with anthropomorphic mounts found on Irish bowls and buckets in Scandinavia, including from Viking graves in Norway. Mirrored human heads are set either side of enamel panels on hanging-bowl escutcheons discovered in a Viking grave at Loland, Norway (Hinds 2009), and mirrored heads are also evident on a mount from another Norwegian grave at Hommersak (ibid.). Three human-shaped escutcheons are present on a hanging-bowl from the River Maas in Holland (MacNamidhe 1989). Probably the most famous of all the anthropomorphic mounts, however, are those from the aristocratic graves of Miklebostad and Oseburg, Norway (ibid.). The former consist of three hanging-bowl escutcheons in the form of a stylised human head over a squared body of *champlevé* enamel with millefiori, with out-turned feet below. (Millefiori is a glasswork technique in which multicoloured glass rods are fused and cut to produce decorative patterns on glassware.) The famous 'Buddha Bucket' from Oseberg consists of a yew bucket, with anthropomorphic handle mounts consisting of a stylised human head over a squared body of vivid yellow and red *champlevé* enamel with millefiori, with the feet crossed in Buddha-style (ibid.).

Probably the best-known parallel for the Ballynapark ladle is the eighth-century Derrynaflan wine-strainer found as part of a hoard near Horse and Jockey, Co. Tipperary, which has very similar dimensions, measuring 378 mm in overall length, with a bowl diameter of 115 mm and a bowl depth of 47 mm (Ó Floinn 1983, 1990). This object is essentially an embellished bronze ladle, which has been further modified through the insertion of a pierced plate into the bowl for use as a wine-strainer (Illus. 10). Hence, it may be regarded as a secular object that has been adapted for liturgical use (Ó Floinn 1983). The straining of wine as part of the Sacrament of the Eucharist would have removed sediment and impurities and clarified the wine.

Illus. 9—The eighth-century, copper-alloy, hanging-bowl mount found at Arnside, Cumbria (courtesy of Kendal Museum).

Illus. 10—The eighth-century Derrynaflan wine-strainer. This object is essentially an embellished bronze ladle, modified through the insertion of a pierced plate into the bowl for use as a wine-strainer (these images are reproduced with the kind permission of the National Museum of Ireland).

However, the small capacity of the Derrynaflan strainer-ladle compared to that of a chalice from the same hoard and the positioning of the straining plate in the bowl may well signify that the purification or straining process was a symbolic rather than a practical one in this instance. Both the Derrynaflan and Ballynapark ladles belong to a long-handled variant, some 26 examples of which are known from early historic contexts in Ireland, Britain and Scandinavia, including many from ninth- and 10th-century graves in Norway and at Birka, in Sweden. The occurrence of at least 11 specimens in Ireland suggests that the type may have developed here (Ó Floinn 1983). The presence of Irish objects, including ladles, in Viking Scandinavian graves not only indicates that these objects travelled with the Vikings, either as loot or traded goods or possibly as gifts and dowry pieces, but also demonstrates that they formed extremely desired and valued possessions of the Scandinavian Vikings.

Illustrations from religious contexts of the ninth and 10th centuries suggest a fashion of using ladles at the time in Ireland (Harbison 1986). In the Book of Kells, at the beginning of St Luke's Gospel, a figure is depicted pouring wine into a chalice, but with a short-handled ladle. Short-handled ladles are also depicted being used to pour water over Pilate's hands on scenes from the Cross of Durrow, Co. Offaly, and St Muiredach's Cross at Monasterboice, Co. Louth (Ó Floinn 1983). An illustration dated to c. AD 870–880, showing the use of a ladle, presumably for holding wine, is incorporated on an elephant ivory plaque held in the Victoria and Albert Museum, London, which was carved in Metz, north-eastern France. The Metz scene shows Mary Magdalene anointing Christ's feet as he sits with his apostles for a meal in the house of Simon the leper at Bethany. A servant offers Christ a beaker with his right hand, probably containing wine, while in his left hand he holds a ladle. The wine has presumably been drawn from a tall, two-handled jar positioned behind the servant (Harbison 1986).

Baptismal scenes on two cross-heads from Durham in England, dated to the 10th century, depict the use of objects that are closer in shape to the Derrynaflan ladle. Harbison (ibid.) adds that these scenes could conceivably raise the possibility of the Derrynaflan ladle having been used for baptismal ceremonies and thereby, with the chalice, having formed a set of sacramental, rather than Eucharistic, vessels.

Christianity was introduced into Ireland mainly from Roman Britain during the fifth century AD. As a result, new object types associated with the Church emerged, such as chalices, patens and containers for the enshrinement of books and relics. It is probable that local native imitations or adaptations were made, chalices and patens being unquestionably the descendants of late Roman domestic tableware (Ryan 1987). Ladles also feature strongly within Late Roman silver hoards in Britain. The fourth-century Mildenhall treasure from Suffolk consisted of silver tableware that included five round-bowled ladles or spoons and eight long-handled spoons (Painter 1977). The round ladles have zoomorphic handles in the form of dolphins. There is a comparable ladle with a dolphin handle from the Traprain Law treasure from East Lothian, Scotland (Curle 1923), which was buried around the middle of the fifth century AD; and there are two sets, each of 10 ladles, from the Hoxne hoard

Fragments of Lives Past

in Suffolk, though not with zoomorphic handles (Bland & Johns 1995). In Roman dining, wine was served throughout the meal as an accompaniment to the food. The Romans mixed their wine with water prior to drinking and typically the wine was mixed to the guest's taste and in his own cup. The wine was poured into the drinking cup with a *simpulum* or ladle, which allowed the server to measure out a specific quantity of wine (Raff 2011).

A bridge between Roman tableware and church plate is demonstrated by a hoard discovered in 1975 during ploughing in a field at Water Newton, in Cambridgeshire, the site of the Roman town of Durobrivae (Painter 1999). The hoard consists of a small gold plaque and 27 silver items, which include jugs, bowls, dishes, a strainer, votive plaques and a two-handled cup or cantharus (a form later used as Christian chalices). Many of the objects bear the monogram formed by the Greek letters *chi* (X) and *rho* (P), the first two letters of Christ's name. The handle of the strainer terminates in a disc and bears the Chi-Rho and the letters *alpha* (A) and *omega* (Ω) (used for 'beginning and end' or 'eternal') within a circle of punched dots. The treasure has been dated to the second half of the fourth century AD and may represent the earliest surviving liturgical plate from the Early Church from anywhere in the Roman Empire. The hoard may have been deposited in response to the persecution of Christians or to more general political instability.

The long-handled ladle is undoubtedly a revered, high-status, secular and ecclesiastical object of the early medieval period, and this is further borne out by its assimilation into Viking contexts from Ireland to Scandinavia. As well as vessels and objects, Irish mounts and fittings travelled with the Vikings and were clearly much appreciated for their decoration, often bright gilding and coloured enamels. A Viking cemetery on Rathlin Island, Co. Antrim, yielded a male skeleton with a silver brooch, a second burial with a sword and a third with a copper ladle, an iron cauldron and copper rings. Much closer to Ballynapark, however, was the discovery in 1900 of a Viking female burial, possibly in Threemilewater townland (Coffey 1902; Bøe 1940; Grogan & Kilfeather 1997), which was accompanied by a pair of Scandinavian gilt-bronze 'tortoise' brooches and a silver chain. Threemilewater is only 6 km north-east of the findspot of the Ballynapark ladle. Other accounts list this Viking burial between Threemilewater and Arklow (Sheehan 1998), which places it even closer to Ballynapark. Threemilewater townland is also the location of an Early Christian establishment associated with St Baothin. St Baothin is said to have been born in AD 536 and is distinguished as having been a student of St Columkille (O'Hanlon 1873). The existence of the Ballynapark ladle may well be related to Viking activity in the area, or to the presence of a significant church site in the vicinity, or both.

A Viking burial accompanied by a bronze ladle was discovered in 1878 in the sandy links at Ballinaby, near the north-western shore of the island of Islay, the southernmost island of the Inner Hebrides of Scotland (Anderson 1880). Islay is merely 32 km off the Antrim coast. This grave contained two burials set a little apart, both with their heads towards the east. One of the graves was that of a Viking warrior accompanied by his sword and other weapons and smithing tools, as well as fragments of a cauldron and what may have been the terminal of a drinking-horn. The second grave was of a female and contained a pair of tortoise brooches, the ladle of beaten bronze and an array of other grave goods, consisting of jewellery and valuable personal items. The ladle may well have been used by this couple to transfer wine or other liquids, perhaps from a bowl into the drinking-horn. The Islay ladle has an overall length of 445 mm, with a bowl diameter of 140 mm and a depth of 89 mm. These dimensions are somewhat larger than the Ballynapark and Derrynaflan examples, but the form of the ladle places it within the long-handled, suggested Irish variant. Anderson (ibid.) noted that to give strength to the handle, the edges were hammered into a T-shaped fillet and that the circular expansion at the end, which he noted as always being perforated in the Roman examples, is filled with a disc hammered up from the underside.

Conclusion

The Ballynapark ladle is a significant finding of a high-status secular and ecclesiastical object, most likely dating from the eighth century AD (Illus. 11). The object type can be seen as an Irish variant that ultimately traces its origin back to late Roman tableware. The Irish ladle subsequently became assimilated into Viking culture and burial across the Irish Sea province, the Scottish Isles and Scandinavia. So why did this prized object end up in boggy ground opposite Jack White's pub? On account of its value, it may well have been concealed for security reasons, with the intention of

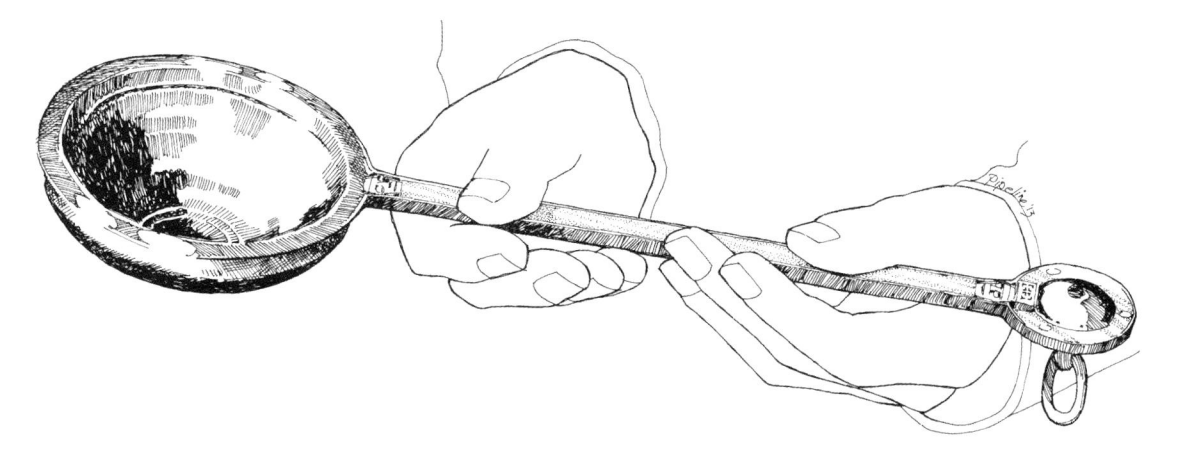

Illus. 11—Reconstruction of the Ballynapark ladle (Dave Pollock).

subsequent retrieval. However, there are other possible explanations. Was it discarded because it was damaged and no longer functional? Was it lost in the bog? Was it a votive offering? Could it have any association with the nearby Viking female burial at Threemilewater, or the ecclesiastical establishment of St Baothin? Perhaps we will never know, but the next time you are serving mixed drink from a punch bowl using a ladle, remember this is a tradition dating back to early historic times.

Acknowledgements

I would like to thank the staff of the National Museum of Ireland for facilitating access to the ladle at Collins Barracks, Dublin, and for their very informative comments and opinions, namely Raghnall Ó Floinn, Mary Cahill, Dr Paul Mullarkey, Carol Smith and Claudia Koehler. Thanks also to Dr Michael Ryan for viewing and discussing the object with me and for very generously sharing his expertise and knowledge, and to Dr Griffin Murray for his expert views and suggestions.

6. Dress and ornament in early medieval Ireland—exploring the evidence

Maureen Doyle

Popular impressions of early medieval Irish dress were originally informed by the study of contemporary texts and images (e.g. O'Curry 1873) (Illus. 1). Modern archaeological studies of the material remains of dress and ornament, however, can contribute significantly to the better understanding of how people in Ireland between the fifth and 12th centuries AD expressed identity through their costume and appearance. This paper will briefly consider some information that can be gleaned from various personal ornaments and how this helps to interpret costume in early medieval Ireland. It draws on the author's doctoral research (Doyle 2010) and, in particular, on relevant archaeological material from excavations on national road schemes.

Illus. 1—A warrior wearing trousers or breeches depicted in the Book of Kells (folio 200r), which dates from the ninth century (The Board of Trinity College Dublin).

Early medieval sources

Texts and images are useful in a number of respects, not least in offering an opportunity to see the 'whole person'. Unlike contemporary Anglo-Saxon or Scandinavian societies, early medieval Irish people buried their dead wrapped in shrouds, rather than fully dressed, so we cannot excavate entire costumes linked to particular people, genders or ages. Texts, including laws, sagas and hagiography (biography of saints), can fill this gap with details of colours, fabrics and ornaments and suggestions as to how and by whom these were used in meaningful ways. Occasional references show such meanings could include uses beyond merely wearing certain items—for example, the eighth-century law-text *Bretha Nemed Tóisech* refers to the use of brooches as legal pledges (Etchingham & Swift 2004, 33), while the 12th-century *Lebor na Cert,* which purports to record the rights of Irish kings, notes that garments such as cloaks, as well as brooches and other ornaments, were offered as royal gifts and tributes (Dillon 1962).

Literary texts use the conventions of the storytellers: repeated motifs depict characters whose social role and status are indicated through details of their appearance and costume. Such idealisation of costume, with a strong focus on high-status individuals, does not, however, represent the whole of society. We might expect more reliable details in the early law-tracts, but these include only occasional details of dress. For example, *Crith Gablach* (a law-tract on social classification) says that the *mruigfer* (the highest grade of noble freeman or strong farmer) and his wife each have four sets of clothes (MacNeill 1923, 291), but gives no detail of them. The greatest detail is found in the 12th-century glosses in *Cáin Iarraith*, the law of fosterage, which specify different coloured garments and precious metal brooches (see Chapter 5, Illus. 8) for the sons of kings, nobles and other ranks (Ní Chonaill 2008, 14); this may reflect distinctions between these grades at all ages. The laws are normative, however, and may not fully reflect what different people actually wore. Similarly, conventions of various literary genres may require that certain items and descriptions are included in the tales, regardless of their social or chronological reality.

Contemporary images also have both uses and limitations. Carved stone, metalwork and illuminated manuscripts depict people in various costumes, usually the *léine* (tunic) and *brat* (cloak), which are described in the texts. This combination of a tunic (which might occur in different lengths and bear a variety of colours and decoration) and a cloak appears to be the quintessential early Irish costume. As far as we can tell, both men and women, and people across different social ranks, wore this costume, although the fact that the images are all from Christian contexts (such as shrines, high crosses and Gospel books) means that they depict a limited range of persons, generally clerics, saints and biblical figures—and these are almost all male (FitzGerald 1997, 253–7). One occasional variation in costume depicted in images (and sometimes mentioned in texts) is the wearing of trousers or breeches, invariably worn by men. Instances such as the warrior in the Book of Kells (Illus. 1) or the soldiers in a scene from Muiredach's cross at Monasterboice, Co. Louth, may suggest that these garments were linked to a particular social role.

Ornaments

Ornaments are the most common material remains of dress and offer insights into the construction and meaning of costume in this period. Irish practice differed from other contemporary European societies, where ornaments were often strongly gendered; in Irish texts and images, however, both men and women wear brooches, pins, arm-rings and other ornaments, albeit sometimes in different ways. According to the seventh-/eighth-century law-tract *Bretha Étgid*, for example, a man was exempt from liability for injuries caused by the pin of his brooch provided he wore it properly, on the shoulder; a woman was supposed to wear her brooch on her breast (Ó Floinn 2001, 1; Kelly 1988, 150; O'Mahony & Richey 1873, 291).

While numerous ornaments of the period survive, focusing on the excavated examples maximises information about their owners and uses. The places where ornaments are found—not just site types, but sometimes very specific contexts, such as the pin and beads from bedding areas at the raised rath at Deer Park Farms, Co. Antrim (Lynn & McDowell 1988, 9)—as well as their occurrence with other types of household goods, and the possibility of scientific dating from the contexts, help us to consider how, when and by whom different items of dress and adornment were used. But many of the known ornaments lack this context. For example, only 36% of 421 brooches studied by the author were excavated (Illus. 2), leaving the vast majority with limited provenance (Doyle 2010). As this is the ornament type most frequently referred to in the texts and shown in images, the lack of context for so many examples is problematic, not least because these 'stray finds' include many of the classic examples of rich metalwork, such as 'The Tara Brooch' from Bettystown, Co. Meath.

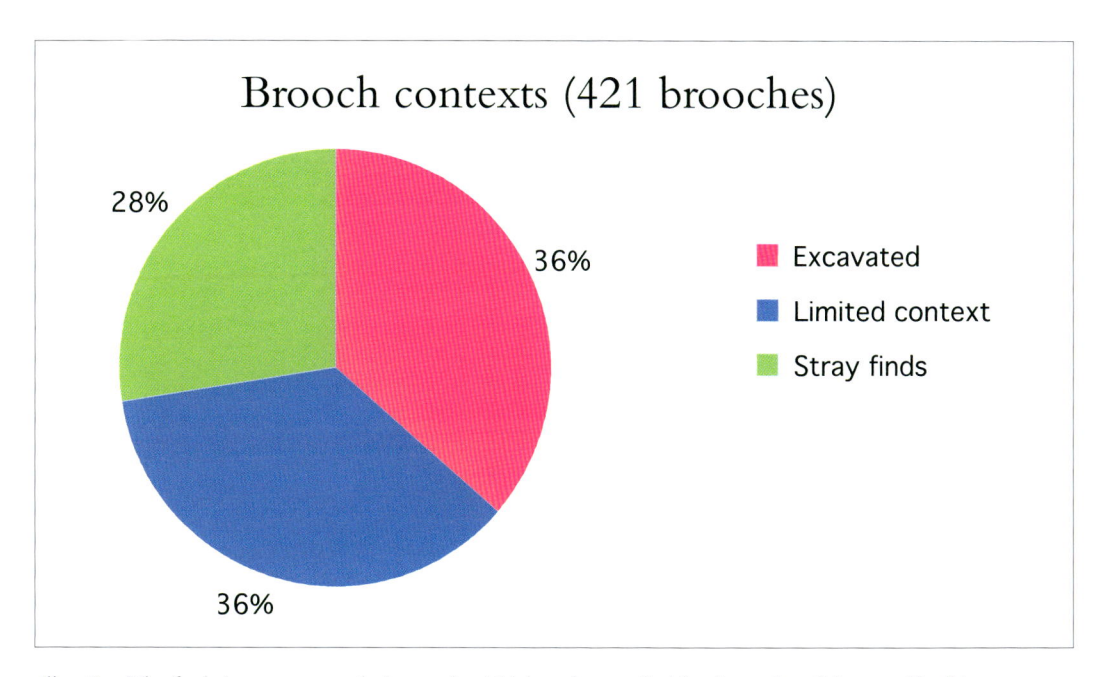

Illus. 2—The find circumstances relating to the 421 brooches studied by the author (Maureen Doyle).

Brooches

Some examples highlight the additional benefits gained from knowing the context from which ornaments were derived. One of the penannular brooches excavated at Castlefarm 1, Co. Meath, a multiperiod enclosed settlement discovered on the M3 motorway, was recovered from a pit (Illus. 3) and the excavator has suggested that it may have been 'purposefully deposited for safe keeping' (O'Connell & Clark 2009, 27; O'Connell 2009, 54). An eighth-century tale, *Echtra Nerai*, refers to valuable items of dress associated with kings (the crown of Briun, the mantle of Loegaire of Armagh and the shirt of Dunlaing in Leinster) being kept in a well and a fairy mound (Cross & Slover 1969, 250, 253). In a broader context, we might consider the suggestion that high-status objects may sometimes have been placed in ritual deposits, rather than disposed of with normal domestic rubbish (Wason 2004, 104). Perhaps the Castlefarm brooch might reflect a similar practice? It is also interesting that radiocarbon dating of charcoal from the pit gave a range of AD 670–890 (Beta-246943, see Appendix 1 for details), providing a *terminus post quem* ('date after which') for the deposition of the brooch (O'Connell & Clark 2009, 27, 63)—a couple of centuries earlier than the dating of similar brooches from the crannogs at Ballinderry I, Co. Westmeath, and Lough Faughan, Co. Down, excavated before the advent of scientific dating.

Two almost identical penannular brooches found within the ditch of an early medieval enclosure and an associated gully at Coonagh West, Co. Limerick (Taylor 2007, 78; Bermingham 2013, 88–9, 100–101), excavated on the Limerick Southern Ring Road, are interesting because the wearing of pairs of brooches (i.e. on either shoulder) is not considered part of Irish costume (Illus. 4). Although retrieved from different contexts, the similar design of these brooches might suggest that they were related in some way in their use. One possibility is that this could suggest an influence from the Anglo-Saxon or earlier Romano-British traditions where women's costume

Illus. 3—A ring-headed pin (top) and a penannular brooch from Castlefarm 1, Co. Meath (John Sunderland).

Illus. 4—The pair of penannular brooches from Coonagh West, Co. Limerick (John Sunderland).

included such paired brooches. Another possibility is that matching pairs of brooches, such as those from Coonagh West or a pair from Ballinderry II, Co. Offaly (Newman 2002, 21), were not worn by a single person, but expressed some other relationship, perhaps of kinship or affiliation, the latter perhaps denoted by royal gifts of ornaments (see above).

Bird-headed penannular brooches excavated at a 'defensive' ringfort at Baronstown, Co. Meath, on the M3, and a cemetery-settlement at Parknahown 5, Co. Laois, on the M7/M8, form part of a small group of just seven similar brooches, most of which were old finds (Ó Floinn 2009). Traditionally these were regarded as Anglo-Saxon types, especially given the known contacts between Ireland and the Anglo-Saxon kingdoms in the early medieval period (see Hencken 1950, 16, 61–4; Linnane & Kinsella 2009, 54). While generally similar brooches occur in both Kent and Yorkshire, often found in burials dated from the later sixth or seventh century (Hirst 1985, 22; Lucy 1998, 58), the Irish brooches are penannular rather than annular in form, and are copper alloy instead of silver. These were not imports from Anglo-Saxon areas, but may have come from Dunadd in Argyll, the early medieval royal centre of the Scottish kingdom of Dál Riada (said to have been founded by settlers from Ireland), where mould fragments for at least six bird-headed penannular brooches were found, dating from the mid- to later seventh century (Lane & Campbell 2000, 106, 239). The Parknahown brooch (Illus. 5) and another brooch from Clogh, Co. Antrim (Youngs 1989, 192), are similar, but not identical, in form to the type of brooch that would have been made using the Dunadd moulds. But brooches of this type might have been made in Ireland, perhaps at the crannog of Moynagh Lough, Co. Meath, where excavations produced a clay mould showing a bird's head terminal, as well as a bird-headed penannular brooch made of sheet metal (Bradley 1994–5, 166; Ó Floinn 2009, 243–5).

Pins

Pins are the most numerous ornaments from early medieval Ireland. They are mentioned in texts, but no contemporary images of them being worn survive. Many different types are known, several of which overlap chronologically; the most common varieties are ring-headed pins (Illus. 3) and stick-pins. Although they were made from a wide variety of materials, scholarship has focused primarily on the metal examples, which can be misleading. The author has analysed over 2,200 stick-pins, nearly one-third of which were non-metallic (Illus. 6) (Doyle 2010). Of these, 95% were made from bone or similar materials and

Illus. 5—The bird-headed penannular brooch from Parknahown 5, Co. Laois (John Sunderland).

the rest are wooden. But all pins shared the same basic function, as garment fasteners, and there are strong similarities in form and decoration across stick-pins, so it should not be assumed that people in the past classified their ornaments on the basis of materials, in the same way as today's scholars often do. Nor should non-metal pins be deemed less attractive. As Hurcombe (2007, 115, 120, 124) pointed out, a range of materials used in the past, including animal bones, could have been perceived as attractive with their gleaming white or cream colour and soft sparkle. Medieval ideas of colour placed greater emphasis on brightness and also on 'lustre, texture, transparency or opacity' (Woolgar 2006, 157). Many sites produce both metal and bone pins. The royal crannog at Lagore, Co. Meath, long regarded as one of the classic high-status sites, yielding richly decorated metal and glass ornaments, also produced 169 bone pins, some of them elaborately decorated, but including 131 plain pig fibula pins (Hencken 1950, 191–4). This co-location of very different materials on a high-status site raises questions about the people who wore the ornaments. While many such sites would have been occupied by a wide range of people, from lords to slaves (O'Sullivan & Nicholl 2011, 61–2, 89), who would presumably have had different access to ornaments and materials, perhaps it is too simplistic to think that different materials were necessarily associated with different ranks of people. Instead, they might reflect the requirements of different social occasions or roles. Possible hints of such distinctions in costume are found in some early texts, including *Bretha im Fhuillema Gell*, which refers to a special garment worn by the king at festivals (Kelly 1988, 166), and *The Wooing of Becfhola*, where a king travelling with just one attendant is wearing only a small brooch, which proves a derisory bride-price (Whitfield 2006, 2–3).

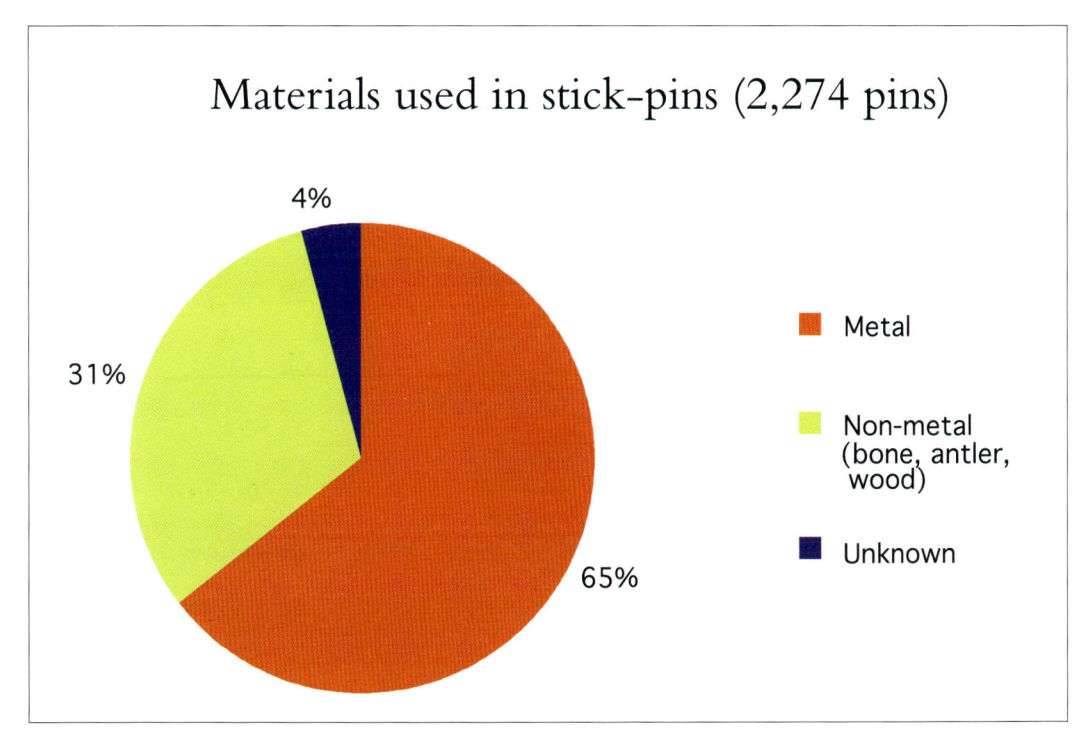

Illus. 6—The materials used in the manufacture of stick-pins (Maureen Doyle).

Bracelets

Textual references to bracelets usually suggest that these were metallic ornaments, but archaeological evidence indicates that a far wider range of materials was used, including jet, lignite, shale, stone, antler, boar tusk and glass, as well as copper alloy, gold and silver. Ornaments of gold and silver are strongly represented in the documentary descriptions and are often discovered in hoards, suggesting that they may have served a function of expressing wealth as well as ornament. However, over two-thirds of bracelets are made of jet/lignite or other forms of fossilised wood (Illus. 7). There are also chronological issues with materials; gold and silver bracelets are strongly associated with the Viking Age (c. AD 800–1150), while the rarer copper-alloy examples span dates from the fourth century through to the Viking Age. Glass bracelets mainly date from the late seventh to the ninth century (Carroll 2001, 101, 105). The more common jet/lignite bracelets, however, were used throughout the entire early medieval period (Lanigan 1964, 60).

Neck-rings

Early texts also refer to metal necklaces, presumably torcs or chains, but few metal neck-rings have been recovered from excavated contexts, as opposed to those known from stray finds or hoards, mostly dating from the Viking Age. Recently, however, a copper-alloy neck-ring was found in a female burial at Ratoath, Co. Meath,

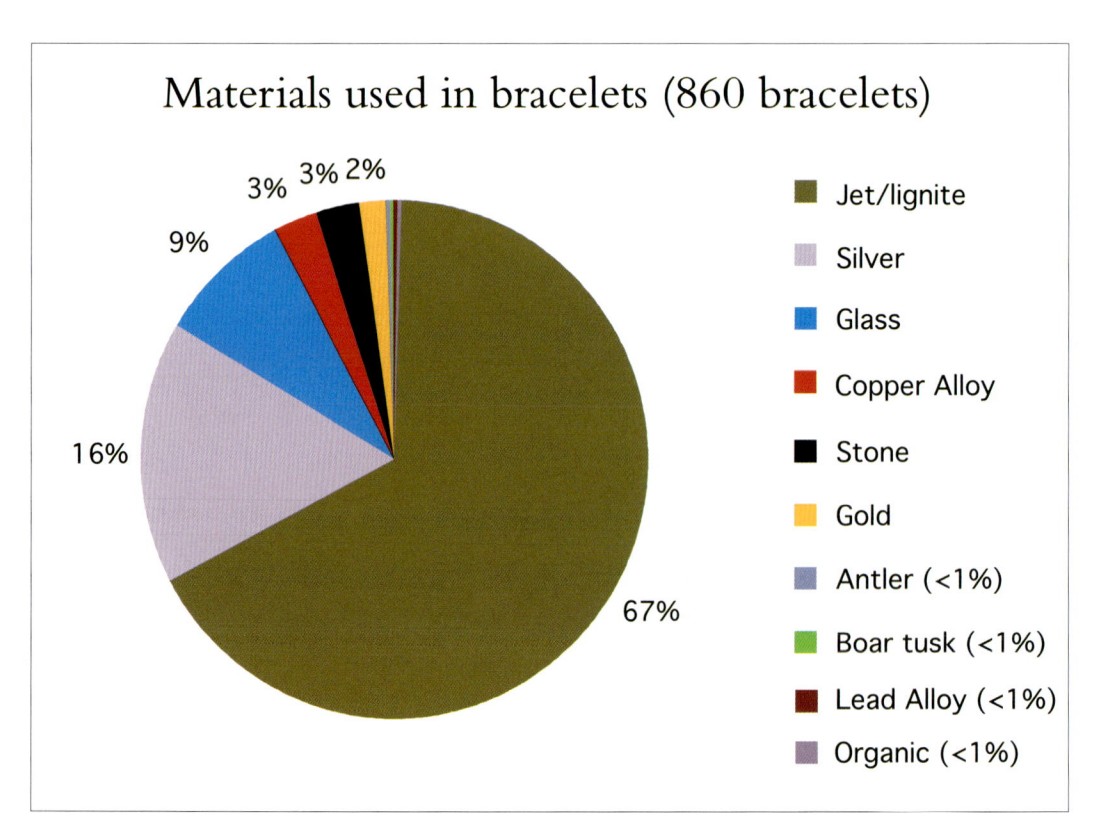

Illus. 7—The materials used in the manufacture of bracelets (Maureen Doyle).

radiocarbon-dated to AD 580–680. This rare artefact showed similarities with a neck-ring from an East Anglian cemetery in Norfolk (O'Brien 2009, 148), leading to suggestions that this might be the burial of an Anglo-Saxon woman; however, stable isotope analysis showed that she was probably local (Wallace 2010, 305–6). This raises questions about her possible links or access to foreign styles and ornaments, and what they meant to her or her people. An excavation of a cemetery-settlement at Owenbristy, Co. Galway, on the N18 Oranmore–Gort road scheme, uncovered an iron tubular neck-ring (Illus. 8) on a crouched male burial, dated to the late sixth/early seventh century (Delaney & Tierney 2011, 186). While different in many details, these two cases confirm that both men and women might wear such ornaments.

Beads

Beads may also have adorned the neck, but are not described in the written sources. Yet beads are a very common find on early medieval sites, suggesting frequent use. The most common material used in their manufacture is glass (Illus. 9), accounting for over 70% of the beads analysed; nearly 90% of all sites on which beads were discovered had glass examples (Doyle 2010). However, this statistic obscures the broader range of materials used, with bone being the second most common, accounting for some 15% of the beads studied. As noted above, we need to consider what early medieval people saw as attractive or ornamental. Other issues relating to beads include questions of how they were used. One might assume they formed necklaces, but of 211 early medieval sites where beads were found, 132 (63%) produced no more than three beads (Illus. 10). At the other end of the spectrum, only eight sites yielded 30 or more

Illus. 8—The iron tubular neck-ring from Owenbristy, Co. Galway (X-ray image by the National Museum of Ireland, photo by John Sunderland).

Illus. 9—Glass beads excavated at Parknahown 5, Co. Laois (John Sunderland).

beads; the largest total from a single site was 163 beads from Lagore, followed by Deer Park Farms with 90 beads. Can beads, where they occur in such small numbers, be representative of necklaces? This might be suggested where beads are excavated in close proximity, for example groups of 16 and eight glass beads, respectively, at Lagore and at Ballinderry II (Hencken 1950, 134; Newman 2002, 111). At Illaunloughan, Co. Kerry, 26 bone beads from a localised area in a midden also suggested a possible necklace (White Marshall & Walsh 2005), while composite bone necklaces were excavated at Whiterath, Co. Louth, and at Clonmacnoise, Co. Offaly (Ó Drisceoil 2001; King 1998). Forty-four bone disc beads found with a female skeleton at Killeany 1, Co. Laois, on the M7/M8, have been interpreted by the excavator as a pater noster (a set of prayer beads) rather than a simple necklace (Illus. 11) (Wiggins 2006a; 2006b; 2009).

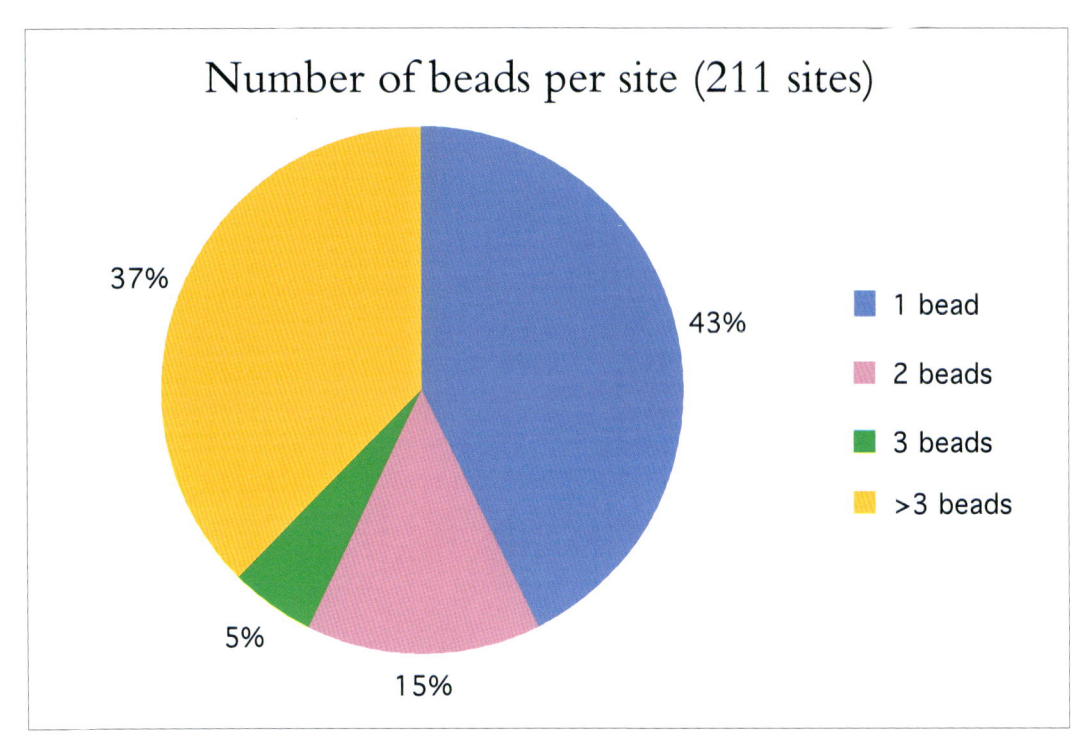

Dress and ornament in early medieval Ireland—exploring the evidence

Illus. 10—The quantity of beads per site (Maureen Doyle).

Illus. 11—The possible pater noster from Killeany 1, Co. Laois (John Sunderland).

77

Beads could also have been used to decorate pins. One find from Lagore comprised a bronze pin with a blue glass bead threaded on to its ring (Hencken 1950, 72, fig. 14 A), while Wilde (1863) referred to an unprovenanced bronze pin with an annular blue glass bead. Excavations at Deer Park Farms produced an iron stick-pin, the head of which was encased in two glass beads fused together (Lynn & McDowell 2011, 332). Beads might also have been used as hair ornaments; some tales, such as *The Destruction of Da Derga's Hostel*, refer to gold beads worn in the hair (Cross & Slover 1969, 94) and this has been suggested as explaining the three glass beads from the head area of a female burial at Parknahown 5 (D Keating, pers. comm.). Finally, instances of single (or occasionally multiple) beads found with infant or child burials excavated on road schemes, as at Camlin, Co. Tipperary, Raystown, Co. Meath, and Parknahown 5 (Flynn 2009, 138; Seaver 2009; O'Neill 2006; 2007; 2008), might reflect their use as protective amulets, rather than decorative ornaments (see O'Brien 1999; Meaney 1981).

A broader picture—assemblages of ornaments

While individual ornaments can tell a story, assessing whole assemblages of such ornaments from excavated sites, and considering the range and combinations of such ornaments, can tell us more. Table 1 shows examples of such combinations of ornaments from a selection of sites excavated on road projects. This gives some idea of the range of different ornaments that are found, and the extent to which they occur. It may also reflect patterns in the distribution of items across site types, which might suggest different uses of costume by people of varying wealth or status, or at different times. Further information could be gained from considering the quantities involved on different sites, which can range from single items to large numbers. For example, the excavation at Castlefarm produced two brooches, 81 pins and six beads, while at the multiperiod settlement at Roestown 2, Co. Meath, also on the M3, 13 beads and at least 67 pins were recovered. Such evaluations of excavated assemblages allow the consideration of issues such as the number and rank of a site's inhabitants, their relative wealth and access to ornaments. One might also consider the use of different elements of costume, for example the use of buckles or of rarer ornament types, such as neck-rings, which might reflect variations in dress, perhaps arising from foreign influences. Studying changes in ornaments over a site's life-span, and making comparisons between assemblages from different site types and geographical regions, can also enhance our knowledge of how people used dress and ornament to express social identity.

Assemblages also show varying combinations of the materials used in ornaments, ranging from precious metals to bone and stone, from exotic to mundane (Table 2). As already noted, simplistic associations of precious metal with high status, or bone and stone with low status, cannot be assumed as such assumptions are unlikely to tell the full story. Occasional textual references to special festive garments (Kelly

Table 1—Selected sites from NRA road scheme excavations, showing variety of ornament types present in dress assemblages (? indicates an uncertain identification).

Site	Brooch	Pin	Bracelet	Finger-ring	Bead	Buckle
Baronstown 1, Co. Meath	X	X	X		X	?
Castlefarm 1, Co. Meath	X	X	X	X	X	
Dowdstown 2, Co. Meath	X	X	X		X	X
Faughart Lower, Co. Louth		X	X		X	X
Johnstown 1, Co. Meath	X	X			X	
Killickaweeny 1, Co. Kildare		X			X	
Leggetsrath West, Co. Kilkenny		X			X	
Newtown, Co. Limerick			X		X	
Newtownbalregan, Co. Louth	X	X			X	
Parknahown 5, Co. Laois	X	X	X		X	X
Rahally, Co. Galway	X			X	X	
Raystown, Co. Meath		X	X	X	X	X
Rochfort Demesne, Co. Westmeath		X			X	X
Roestown 2, Co. Meath		X	X		X	X
Twomileborris, Co. Tipperary		X			X	?

Table 2—Selected sites from NRA road scheme excavations, showing variety of materials used in ornament assemblages.

Site	Silver	Copper alloy	Iron	Bone/antler	Glass	Lignite	Stone	Other
Baronstown 1, Co. Meath		X	X	X	X			
Castlefarm 1, Co. Meath	X	X	X	X	X	X	X	
Dowdstown 2, Co. Meath		X	X	X	X	X		
Faughart Lower, Co. Louth		X	X	X	X	X		
Johnstown 1, Co. Meath		X	X	X	X			
Killickaweeny 1, Co. Kildare		X	X	X	X			
Leggetsrath West, Co. Kilkenny		X			X			
Newtown, Co. Limerick					X			
Newtownbalregan, Co. Louth		X			X			
Parknahown 5, Co. Laois		X		X	X	X		
Rahally, Co. Galway		X			X			Pewter
Raystown, Co. Meath		X	X	X	X	X	X	
Rochfort Demesne, Co. Westmeath		X		X	X			
Roestown 2, Co. Meath		X	X	X	X	X		Amber
Twomileborris, Co. Tipperary		X		X	X			

1988, 166) or to a king wearing only a small brooch instead of his expected finery (Whitfield 2006, 2) remind us that individuals might vary their dress and ornament depending on circumstances. Multiple materials may also reflect people's access to different resources or to the services of craftworkers, or indeed indicate a person's ability to make their own ornaments from readily available materials, such as bone. Again, detailed studies of variations and chronologies add to the picture of the perceptions and choices of early medieval people.

Conclusion

The material relating to dress and ornament that has been recovered in recent years from pre-development archaeological excavations has significant potential to increase our understanding of dress in early medieval Ireland. Exploring a variety of approaches to their study, such as those mentioned above, will offer new insights not just into how people dressed and adorned themselves, but into the meanings associated with dress and appearance during this period, and what this can tell us about social identities.

Acknowledgements

This paper draws on elements of the author's Ph.D research, which was funded by a University College Dublin (UCD) Ad Astra Research Scholarship, supported by the UCD Humanities Institute, and supervised by Dr Aidan O'Sullivan of the School of Archaeology, UCD. Matt Seaver, Cóilín Ó Drisceoil and Heather King kindly provided unpublished information on particular ornaments.

7. Early medieval E ware pottery: an unassuming but enigmatic kitchen ware?

Ian W Doyle

Unusually, the large-scale production or demand for pottery vessels ceased after the later Bronze Age (c. 500 BC) in Ireland. During the subsequent Iron Age (500 BC–AD 400) and into the early medieval period (AD 400–1169) there was no longer an interest in pottery manufacture (see McCutcheon, Chapter 8), even though the need for ceramic crucibles for metal-working ensured some expertise continued in the working of clay vessels at high temperatures. The recent spate of archaeological excavations has done little to alter this picture, such that the late Professor Barry Raftery's (1995) paper on the absence of pottery from Iron Age Ireland has not been challenged to any significant degree. It thus seems that the availability of robust wooden or metal containers, the use of animal skin bags/sacks, or a preference for roasting foods without ceramics, as well as a move away from using pottery to accompany burials, effectively removed ceramics from the Irish archaeological record.

When we do see pottery being manufactured on any notable scale, it is mainly concentrated in the north-east of Ireland, in particular in counties Antrim, Down and north Louth. This is, of course, the handmade tradition of Souterrain Ware, in the shape of flat-bottomed, straight-sided pots and bowls that generally date from the mid-seventh to the 12th centuries AD (Armit 2008, 8; Dunlop 2013; O'Sullivan et al. 2014, 240–2). Only in the Hiberno-Norse towns of Dublin and Waterford during the 10th century do we see the beginnings of the frequent use of pottery, in this case comprising imports from Britain and the Continent.

During the period spanning the mid-fifth to seventh centuries AD, small quantities of pottery were imported into Ireland and western Britain from the eastern Mediterranean, North Africa and western Gaul (modern-day France). The ceramics from the Mediterranean that made their way here take the form of amphorae containing wine or olive oil, as well as late Roman fine ware dishes. This paper will concentrate on the material from western Gaul—a range of pottery referred to by archaeologists as E ware or Class E (Illus. 1). This pottery has been recovered from some 50 sites in Ireland, including some excavated in advance of recent motorway construction, particularly in north Leinster. This short paper sets out the current state of knowledge on this pottery type and what we have learned about it from some of the NRA-funded excavations.

What is E ware?

E ware is an unglazed, undecorated and unpainted coarse pottery. Its fabric is hard and gritty, with occasional large pieces of white quartz, and an exterior surface that looks

Fragments of Lives Past

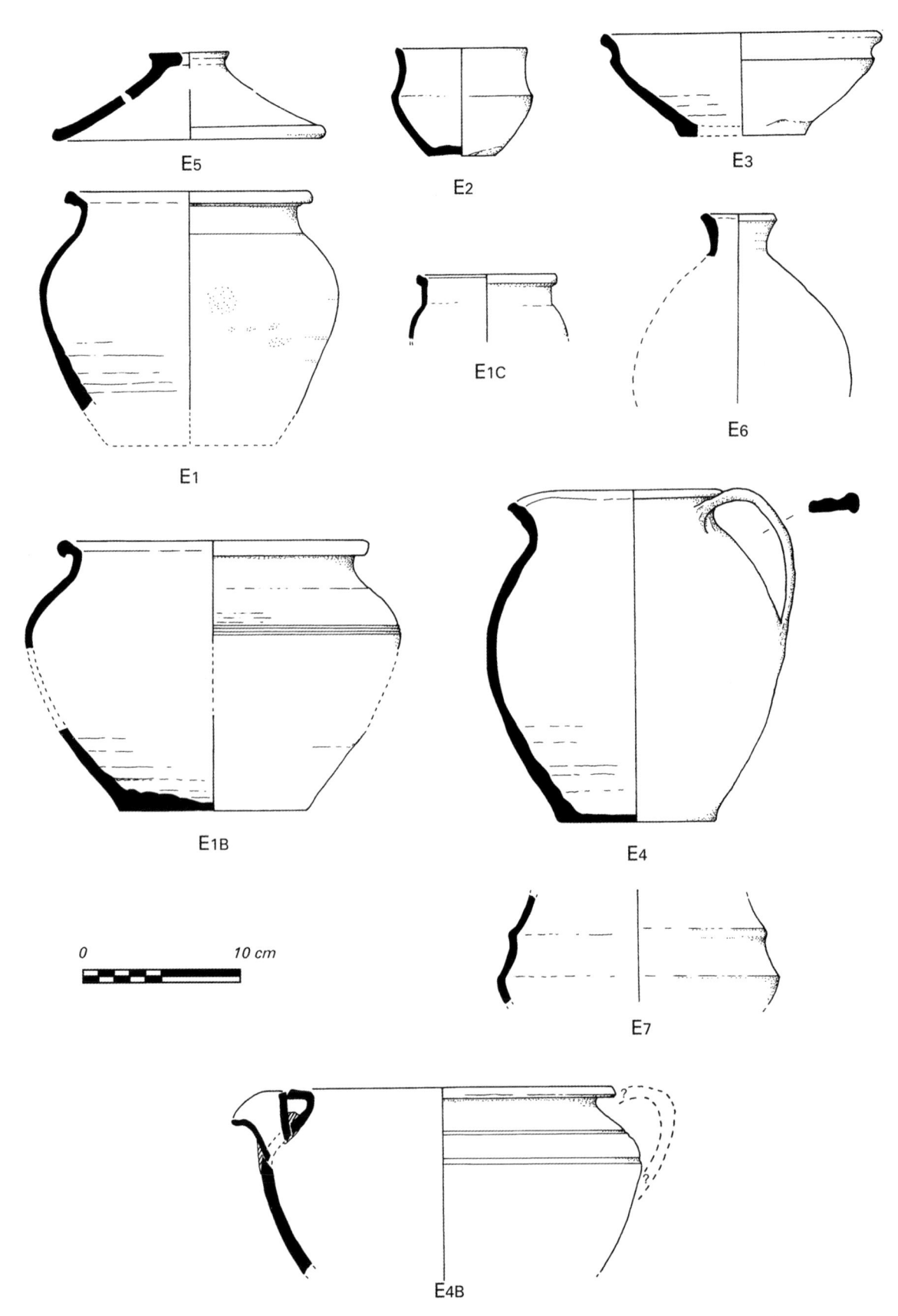

Illus. 1—The range of E ware pottery forms includes pots, beakers, bowls, jugs and lids (from Campbell 2007).

as if it was wiped or sponged when still wet (Illus. 2). This latter effect gives the outer surfaces an appearance that has been previously described as 'pimply'. It is wheel-made and the colour varies from grey, black, red, white-cream to brown, although it is generally light-brown to grey (Illus. 3). In short, it is not a prepossessing type of pottery, yet it is the most frequently recovered imported pottery type from early medieval western Britain and Ireland. E ware occurs in a range of forms, including jars (E1), beakers (E2), bowls (E3), jugs (E4) and lids (E5) (see Illus. 1). Most of the fragments found in Ireland appear to be from jars, although in some cases it can be difficult to be precise about the original forms once a vessel is broken and dispersed. In many cases only a single sherd or a handful of fragments of individual vessels are recovered by excavation.

E ware has a wide distribution in south-west Britain, southern Wales, the Isle of Man, western Scotland and the north-eastern, eastern, southern and midland parts of Ireland (Illus. 4). Unlike the Mediterranean ceramic material, which is mainly concentrated in south-west Britain and which has been linked to a foreign interest in Cornish tin (Thomas 1988), western Gaulish E ware has a more pronounced Irish distribution. Approximately 50 archaeological excavations in Ireland, mostly settlements, have recovered this pottery to date.

Yet why is E ware important? In the days before the widespread use of radiocarbon dates, pottery was used to date archaeological deposits. This was particularly important in Ireland, given that coinage was non-existent at this period and there were no other common types of pottery to act as a chronological indicator. This has now changed owing to the use of radiocarbon dating on almost every archaeological excavation (see below). The other reason of interest is that imported ceramics offer a unique insight into foreign contacts and the role of trade. In a time of considerable social and economic change, for example the adoption of Christianity and the emergence of the dispersed settlement pattern represented by the ringfort (Kerr & McCormick 2014), this is quite important.

Unfortunately, our understanding of the point of origin of E ware is somewhat unclear, though western France is likely, as vessels in similar fabrics are known from some post-Roman sites in this area—in Bordeaux, in particular, and in the regions of the Touraine, Saintonge and Poitou, north of Bordeaux, or the general area between the Loire and the Gironde rivers (Wooding 1996, 77–8; Campbell 2007, 48–9). It is worth remarking that even the name for this pottery type—E ware—is an admission of a lack of clarity, and after more than 60 years of study it can still be seen as a provisional name. In the 1950s, when the names for imported pottery types were standardised, A ware, B ware and D ware were similarly used as a shorthand for three distinct classes of pottery. These names have been largely superseded, and we now know these as African Red Slipware and Phocaean Red Slipware (the former A wares), Late Roman Amphora(e) (LRA) 1, 2 and 3 (the former B wares) and DSPA or *Dérivées sigillées paléochrétiennes groupe Atlantic* (the former D ware) (Doyle 2009). Yet, E ware stubbornly remains with its alphabetic mnemonic. In 1990 Charles Thomas (1990, 22), who created this classification during the 1950s, posed the origins of

Illus. 2—The fabric of E ware varies in colour, but generally has a 'pimply' appearance where inclusions in the fabric protrude slightly. This example is from Caherlehillan, Co. Kerry (courtesy of John Sheehan, University College Cork).

Illus. 3—Sherds from E ware jars from excavations at Roestown 2 and Castletown Tara 1, Co. Meath, on the M3 motorway (Ian Doyle).

84

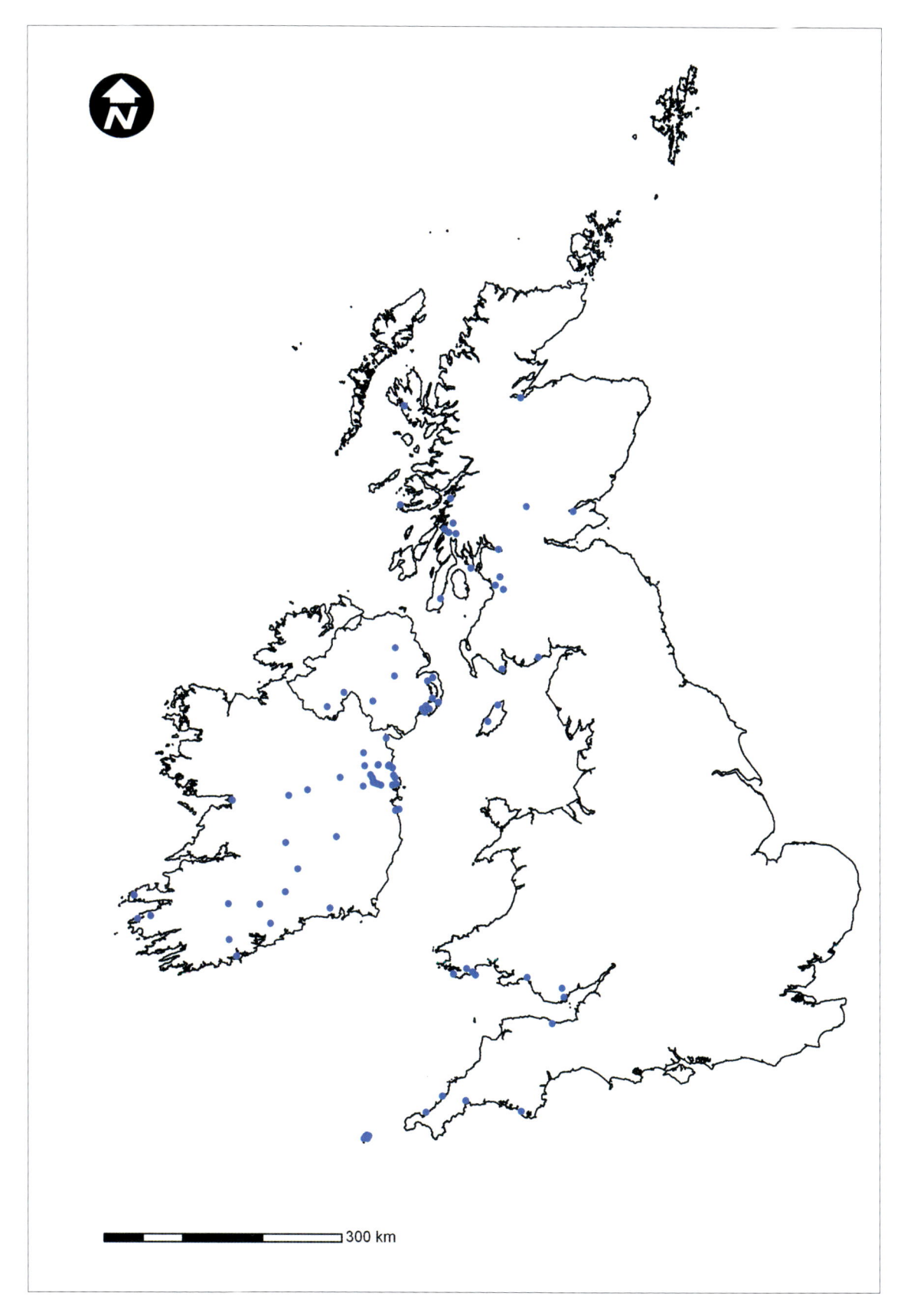

Illus. 4—The distribution of E ware in Ireland and western Britain (after Doyle 2009 and Campbell 2007).

E ware as a challenge, but almost 25 years on we are no closer to divining where precisely in France this pottery was manufactured. Yet, just as in Ireland, where the increase in archaeological excavations during the late 20th century and early years of the new millennium saw vast amounts of new archaeological data being generated, it does seem likely that the recent campaigns of excavation in late and post-Roman French towns will eventually provide a more precise context, and possibly even a new name, for this type of pottery.

While the Late Roman Amphorae (LRA) of the fifth and sixth centuries AD were traded because of their wine and olive oil contents, E ware was a likely accompaniment to wine in wooden casks and possibly with other perishable goods (Thomas 1990). An alternative view, advanced by Campbell (2007), is that E ware should not be seen as a kitchen ware, but as a range of containers for goods. A red dyestuff from the plant Dyer's Madder has been identified as the commodity contained within one vessel (Walton Rogers 2005), but the suggestion has also been made that E ware may have been used for trading nuts, spices and honey as well as other 'exotic luxury goods' (Campbell 2007, 49–52). While a programme of scientific residue sampling may help address this issue (see Smyth & Evershed, Chapter 1, for an example relating to Neolithic pottery), the Irish evidence is of interest owing to the frequency in which the E5 lid form occurs.

The E ware E5 lids are conical in shape, with an increase in body thickness towards a central raised boss or handle grip (see Illus. 1). A groove or seat to accommodate a lid is a feature on many E1 rim sherds, and fragments of E5 lids are known from Dalkey Island, Mount Offaly and Balrothery Rosepark, Co. Dublin, and Ninch, Kiltrough and Site M at Knowth, Co. Meath, as well as Ballycatteen, Co. Cork, Clogher, Co. Tyrone and Caherlehillan, Co. Kerry (Doyle 2009, fig. 4). A further example of an E5 lid is known from Bar Point, St Mary's, the largest island of the Isles of Scilly, off the south-west coast of Cornwall (Campbell 2007, fig. 33). Where the central boss of the lid survives, a small central perforation is present in the boss. The piercing of such lids was presumably to enable the release of steam during cooking, a feature found in the general late Roman pottery repertoire. This suggests that we should not discount a role for E ware as a kitchen ware rather than seeing it exclusively as a container.

Chronology

In 1979 archaeologist Richard Warner argued that there was a chronological separation between sherds of Mediterranean LRA 1 and 2 (Bii and Bi or B ware amphorae) and sherds of E ware based on the sequence of deposits encountered at the royal hillfort of Clogher, Co. Tyrone. Sherds of LRA 1 and 2 were found in the lower fills of the Clogher enclosure ditch, which were sealed by a layer of sterile clay (the 'Clogher Yellow Layer'). Only E ware was recovered from the fills overlying the Clogher Yellow Layer (Warner 1979; 1985–6). While this stratigraphic sequence is not in doubt at Clogher, information from other Irish sites has since altered the idea of a clear, and neat, chronological separation between Mediterranean LRA sherds and E ware. At several sites, both Mediterranean and Gaulish wares have been recovered from the same deposits: these include Caherlehillan, Co. Kerry, Colp West, Co. Meath, and Dalkey Island, Co. Dublin (Doyle 1998; 2009; Sheehan 2009). Similarly, at Whithorn, in Galloway, Scotland, Mediterranean ceramics and E ware were found in a series of excavated deposits dated to c. AD 550 (Hill 1997, 323–4), while at Bantham, South Devon, and Tintagel, Cornwall, recent radiocarbon dating points to Mediterranean LRA sherds in contexts dating from the early seventh century (i.e. a little later than traditionally accepted) (Reed et al. 2011; Barrowman et al. 2007, 332). What this suggests is that the picture is a little more untidy than the neat arrangement demonstrated in the sequence of deposits at Clogher hillfort. It would appear that Mediterranean and Gaulish wares overlapped chronologically somewhere around the middle of the sixth century AD and that the use of Mediterranean amphorae may have extended into the early seventh century.

That said, there are issues with dating pottery, as there is the likelihood of residuality where vessels, or even sherds, can be retained (or 'curated') in active use over a prolonged period or that sherds may be redeposited in later contexts. Moreover, E ware vessel shapes do not seem to have changed through time (thus there is no stylistic sequence) and, of course, there is no detailed understanding of the place of this pottery in French archaeological deposits. Finally, there are few direct radiocarbon dates that relate to individual sherds, such as from matching deposits or from organic residues attached to sherds. Even so, how does recent evidence from Ireland sit with this picture?

What have we learned from Roestown 2, Collierstown 1 and Raystown?

In keeping with many other classes of archaeological sites or artefacts, the rate of discovery of this pottery, as shown in Illus. 5, shows a marked increase during the early years of the new millennium. This is in part due to the construction of new roads and motorways, but also the other forms of development, such as the housing, gas pipelines and commercial developments that characterised the 'Celtic Tiger' period of Ireland's economic experience. The crude implication from this in terms of this paper is that as archaeological excavation techniques advanced from the 1930s to the present, there should have been a rise in the quality of excavated evidence (i.e. more frequent use of scientific dating evidence, more palaeoenvironmental data, better stratigraphic evidence, etc.). A summary analysis of three NRA-funded excavations is interesting in this regard.[1]

---

[1] Roestown 2: NGR 295793, 253824; height 106 m OD; Excavation Reg. No. E3055; Ministerial Direction No. A008; Excavation Director Rob O'Hara.
Collierstown 1: NGR 294743, 258825; height 112 m OD; Excavation Reg. No. E3068; Ministerial Direction No. A008; Excavation Director Rob O'Hara.
Raystown: NGR 304976, 251474; height 71 m OD; Excavation Licence No. 03E1229 extension; Ministerial Direction No. A011; Excavation Director Matthew Seaver.

Fragments of Lives Past

These three sites are in County Meath and comprise Roestown 2, Collierstown 1 and Raystown. Each of these sites produced small amounts of E ware (one or two vessels per site) and each was also well provided for in terms of radiocarbon dates. As a whole, this provides an opportunity to look at the chronology of this pottery in the north Leinster area. That this is an issue of some interest is borne out by the role pottery played in dating the nearby royal crannog of Lagore, some 2 km east of Dunshaughlin, Co. Meath, where the presence of E ware in Phases 1a and 1b is seen as marking the beginning of activity at this site, c. AD 600 (Hencken 1950; Warner 1985–6). This internationally important site was excavated in the 1930s by the Harvard Archaeological Expedition and is in relatively close proximity to the three recently excavated sites mentioned above in the early medieval kingdom of southern Brega (Illus. 6).

The Roestown 2 archaeological site (Illus. 7) was a large, multiple-enclosure settlement, approximately 2 km north of Dunshaughlin, which was excavated in advance of the construction of the M3 motorway (O'Hara 2009a). Four sherds of E ware, representing two E1 pots, were recovered from Enclosures 1 and 2, which were assigned to Phase 1A, the earliest stage in the occupation of the site. Cattle bone from this phase of activity on the site was radiocarbon-dated to AD 530–650 and the excavator's view was that the E ware from Enclosure 2 related to this phase of activity, but had been disturbed (O'Hara 2009a, 62, 65). Additional sherds from Enclosure 2 were not associated with radiocarbon dates, but were also attributed to the same phase. Interestingly, other radiocarbon dates from this phase extended from

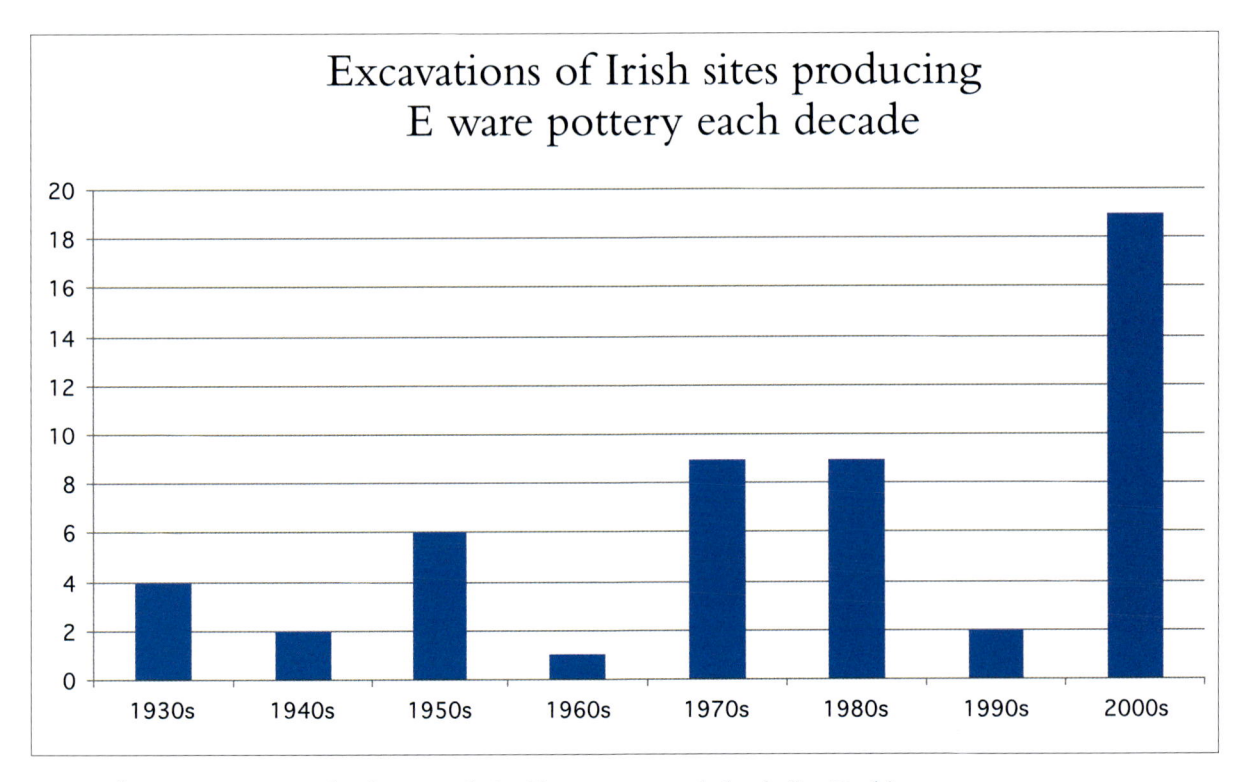

Illus. 5—Excavations of Irish sites producing E ware pottery each decade (Ian Doyle).

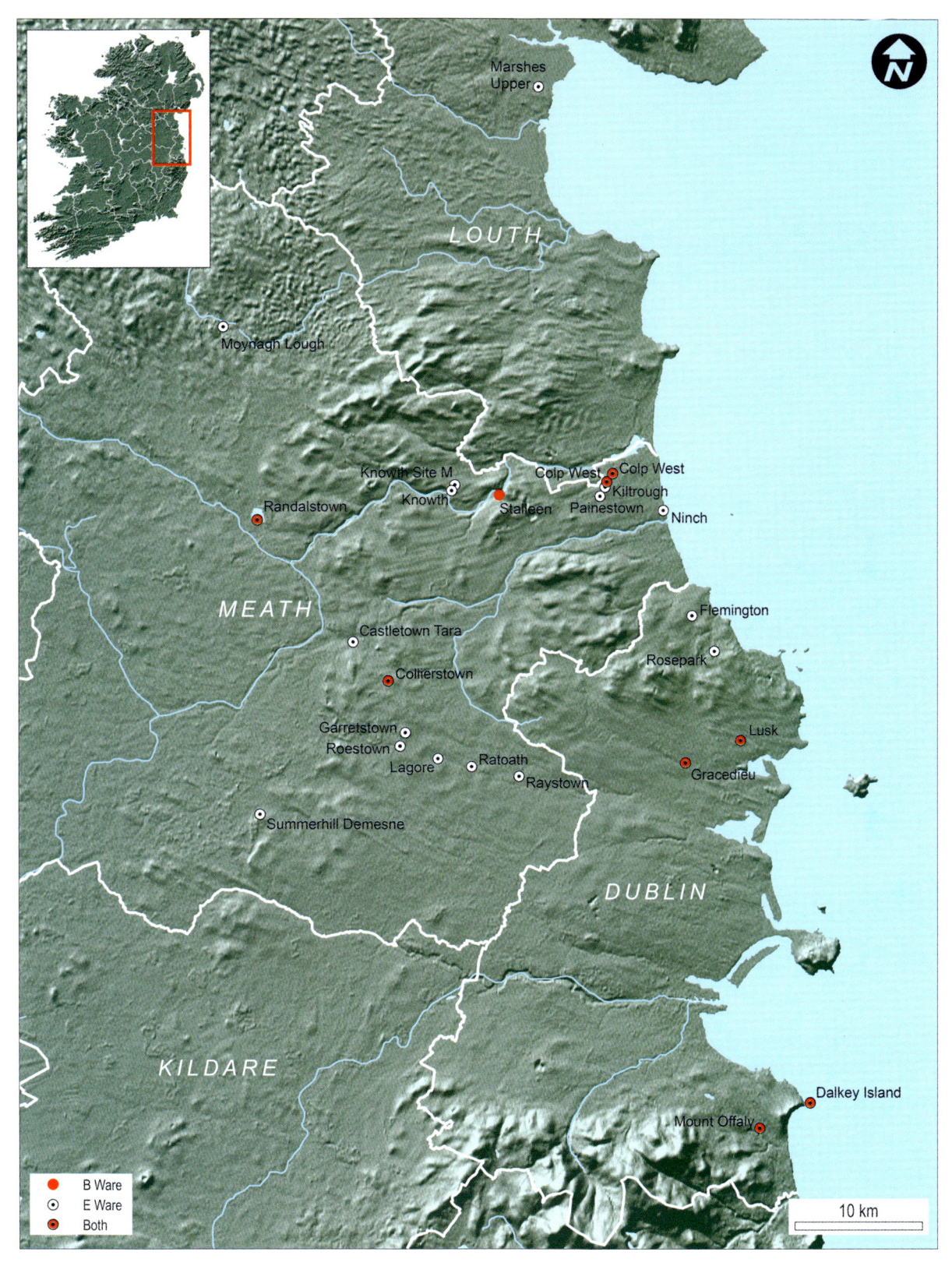

Illus. 6—The distribution of E ware in north Leinster, showing the location of Collierstown 1, Roestown 2, Raystown and Lagore in County Meath (Ian Doyle).

Illus. 7—Post-excavation aerial view of Roestown 2, Co. Meath (Studio Lab).

the eighth to 10th centuries AD, demonstrating the longevity of occupation at this site. If we accept the dating assigned to the earliest phase based on the radiocarbon date cited above, this is broadly in accordance with the established date range for E ware of mid-sixth to late seventh century AD.

The sequence of activity at Collierstown 1, a late Iron Age/early medieval enclosed cemetery, was equally complex (O'Hara 2009b; 2009c) (Illus. 8). This site, also excavated on the M3 motorway, was approximately 3 km east of the Hill of Tara and 5 km north of Roestown 2. Significantly, the imported pottery from this site is from a funerary context, whereas the majority of finds of imported wares in Ireland are from a settlement context (Doyle 2009). Collierstown 1 produced sherds from an eastern Mediterranean Phocaean Red Slipware bowl and from an amphora (LRA 1 or Bii) from the Phase 1 and Phase 2 enclosure ditches. The Phase 2 ditch produced a sherd of E ware in a ditch fill (F69) that also contained a sherd of LRA 1 (Illus. 9). Context F69 was identified by the excavator as a fill of a recut in the ditch and was stratigraphically later than another fill (F67) that returned a radiocarbon date of AD 420–610 (Beta-247009; see Appendix 1 for details). Other dates indicate activity into the seventh century. In general, at Collierstown 1 we can see the presence of Mediterranean wares across the site in ditch deposits dating from the fifth to sixth centuries AD (e.g. the Phase 2 ditch F196.) The single sherd of E ware was in the same deposit as a sherd of LRA 1 and hence lacks any neat chronological or phasing separation from this pottery,

Illus. 8—Post-excavation aerial view of Collierstown 1, Co. Meath (Studio Lab).

yet it does have a later bias than the bulk of the Mediterranean wares on the site. Yet again, the evidence does not challenge the established dating of E ware.

The site at Raystown excavated in advance of the construction of the M2 motorway, near Ashbourne, was another large, high-status settlement (Illus. 10) where two sherds of E ware from an E1 pot were found. This was a farming and milling complex with a burial ground at its core (Seaver 2006; 2010). The initial phase of early medieval activity saw the digging of a shallow, penannular enclosure ditch that acted as the focus for a cemetery. An early fill in this ditch contained cereal remains, which were radiocarbon-dated to AD 410–560 (O'Sullivan & Stanley 2006, 134). A sherd of E ware was found in an upper (i.e. later) fill within this ditch. During this phase burials were placed within and around the penannular ditch, and bone from one of the burials cutting into the ditch fills was dated to AD 430–610 (ibid.). This suggests that this ditch was backfilled by the end of the sixth century and that the sherd of E ware was deposited during this late sixth-century/early seventh-century horizon.

Discussion

The brief look at chronology offered here suggests that E ware adheres to the core range of dates now assigned to it (i.e. the mid-sixth to late seventh century). It is

Fragments of Lives Past

Illus. 9—A rim sherd from an eastern Mediterranean Phocaean Red Slipware bowl (left) and a sherd of E ware from Collierstown 1 (John Sunderland).

Illus. 10—A reconstruction of the settlement at Raystown, Co. Meath, c. AD 900 (Simon Dick).

likely that E ware was circulating in the north Leinster area in the mid-sixth century and this could pull the dating of the phases cited by Warner (1985–6) at Lagore back marginally into the mid-sixth century, as opposed to the date of c. AD 600. A more comprehensive analysis of recent radiocarbon dates across a wider range of sites could prove useful, yet due care needs to be exercised given the windows of time provided by such dates, the possibility of redeposition and curation of pottery, and the fact that few excavators are minded to radiocarbon date a context that produces a solitary sherd of pottery.

Nonetheless, a comprehensive dating analysis would still be a useful exercise. The presence of this imported ceramic type in a formative part of the early medieval period is also worth noting. In a recent paper, McCormick (2013) has pointed to the late seventh/eighth century AD as a key period of change. During this time mill-building begins to increase and large numbers of small grain-drying kilns give way to smaller numbers of larger ones. The analysis of a range of radiocarbon dates by McCormick appears to point to a relative decrease in the rate of ringfort construction (or radiocarbon dates from this period) at a point where it has been suggested that the reciprocal economy and its associated exchange of prestige goods, such as imports, gave way to one based on agricultural surpluses and traded commodities (ibid.; Kerr & McCormick 2014). So, just at this point where Irish social and economic developments are becoming recognisable, albeit perhaps imperfectly, the trade represented by E ware seems to disappear, or at least the tangible ceramic marker of such trade is no longer present in the archaeological record. The enigmatic nature of E ware, insofar as we have little or no understanding of its place in western French ceramic sequences, means that the Continental background to this trade and the context for its beginning and end are unclear at present, pending fieldwork and greater international collaboration. As the title of this paper suggests, this pottery type is unassuming in not being provided with a pleasing surface treatment, decoration or a fine fabric, yet it remains an enigma in terms of its precise point of origin and the background to its exchange.

Acknowledgements

The author would like to thank the editors for their comments on this paper and the many archaeologists who have provided access to excavated material. Finally, I would like to thank Robert Shaw of the Discovery Programme for assistance with Illus. 6.

8. In praise of Leinster Cooking Ware
Clare McCutcheon

The background

For over 1,000 years, from the end of the Bronze Age in the eighth century BC to the Viking Age in the ninth century AD, there was an almost complete lack of pottery on the island of Ireland. The country had not been settled by the Romans in the Iron Age and so the everyday use of a wide variety of pottery, so common on the Continent and in England, was lacking here. That pottery was not unknown in Ireland is evidenced by the small quantities of imported B ware and E ware (see Doyle, Chapter 7) during the fifth to eighth centuries AD, but the alternatives of wood, leather and metal more than adequately fulfilled the requirements of the people. The presence of Vikings in the ninth and 10th centuries, largely of Norwegian origin, did not affect this situation as they too were largely aceramic. Later 10th- and 11th-century excavated levels in the cities of Dublin, Cork, Waterford and Wexford contained unglazed wares from south-east England and some glazed wares from eastern England and the Continent, primarily France and Belgium.

The first locally made wares in Ireland are the ninth-century Souterrain Ware of the north-east and the mid-12th-century Leinster Cooking Ware of the east and south-east. Both are unglazed, hand-built wares, although Souterrain Ware closely mirrors prehistoric wares in bucket shape, while Leinster Cooking Ware is typical of the contemporary shape in Britain and the Continent, with a rounded body and everted or flared rim. The official arrival of the Anglo-Normans in the latter part of the 12th century saw the production, into an open market, of glazed wares based on the familiar prototypes from Bristol. The Dublin Guild Merchant Roll indicates at least 40 names directly associated with pottery and tile-making in the city from c. 1190 to 1265. The documentary, archaeological and stylistic evidence indicates that glazed pottery was made in Dublin from c. 1180 onwards. The increasing amount of medieval pottery recovered during excavations in Kilkenny also indicates a locally made glazed ware in production here from the late 12th century.

Alongside these developments in the production and use of glazed wares, Leinster Cooking Ware remained in constant production for some 200 years. Visually it would not have been as exciting as the shiny greens and browns of the glazed wares, but it appears to have filled a considerable niche in the market with a wide range of vessel types fulfilling a variety of roles. It was used in conjunction with wooden, metal and leather vessels but, as ever, the value of pottery across all sites and all time periods is robustness. Even broken and worn, pottery does not require the anaerobic conditions necessary for the survival of wood and leather, while metal vessels tended to be melted down for re-casting and so do not survive in great numbers.

It is also true to say that pottery in general was not highly valued in the medieval period. In a period with little disposable income and less small coin circulating, the investment in the production and distribution of vessels was not to be undertaken lightly and a secure market was essential to repay the time and talents invested. Even imported pottery, so highly regarded in modern times, was not registered in the customs dues of the time, being grouped together with many other small items that were of so little value, it was deemed unnecessary to quantify or charge for them by name. There is a misunderstanding that imported French pottery was traded into Ireland as a separate commodity, for example, when in fact it most likely came in as an advertising ploy along with the wines of the time. Excavations have revealed that in 13th-century Cork, up to 60% of the pottery was imported from France, in contrast to only 15% in Dublin. The shallow, turbulent nature of the River Liffey led to poor access to the centre of Dublin. As imported goods would have had to be double-handled (i.e. unloaded from sea-going vessels into smaller boats for transport into the city centre), it made sense to develop a local pottery production as soon as possible. In addition, the political situation in Dublin and its hinterland was much more stable than in other parts of the country and it would have been safe to set up pottery production outside the protection of the city limits. In contrast, both Cork and Waterford were slow to develop local pottery production as the river access to the city centres was outstanding, with sea-going vessels unloading directly onto the quaysides, allowing for minimal handling of the occasional baskets of fragile pottery that accompanied the barrels of wine.

Leinster Cooking Ware

Leinster Cooking Ware was originally defined by archaeologist Raghnall Ó Floinn (1976; 1988). The actual term Leinster Cooking Ware is loaded with functional overtones. The term was chosen for this unglazed ware as the majority of the vessels excavated by the mid-1970s were cooking vessels, but subsequent excavations throughout the 1990s and 2000s, primarily at Carrickmines Castle in south Dublin (Illus. 1),[1] have substantially increased the relative quantity of other vessels, such as jugs, platters and lamps (Breen 2013). It is clear that many of the vessels made in this fabric were never used for cooking, although they could withstand heat from a fire. For example, many of the jugs also show evidence of being used over or beside a flame and, while not used for cooking, they were probably used for heating liquid, such as wine. The wine of the medieval period quickly went off and was more usually drunk diluted and spiced with herbs—something similar to our mulled wine.

Leinster Cooking Ware is coarse-grained in appearance, with visible mica platelets and quartz. It is unglazed, often thin-walled and can be black or shades of brown. The base of every vessel is marked with a gritty surface, most likely from being hand-built on a bed of sand. The benefits of this unpromising appearance, however, are in

---

[1] NGR 321877, 224036; height 65–70 m OD; Excavation Licence Nos 00E0525 & 02E1532; Excavation Directors Mark Clinton & Gary Conboy.

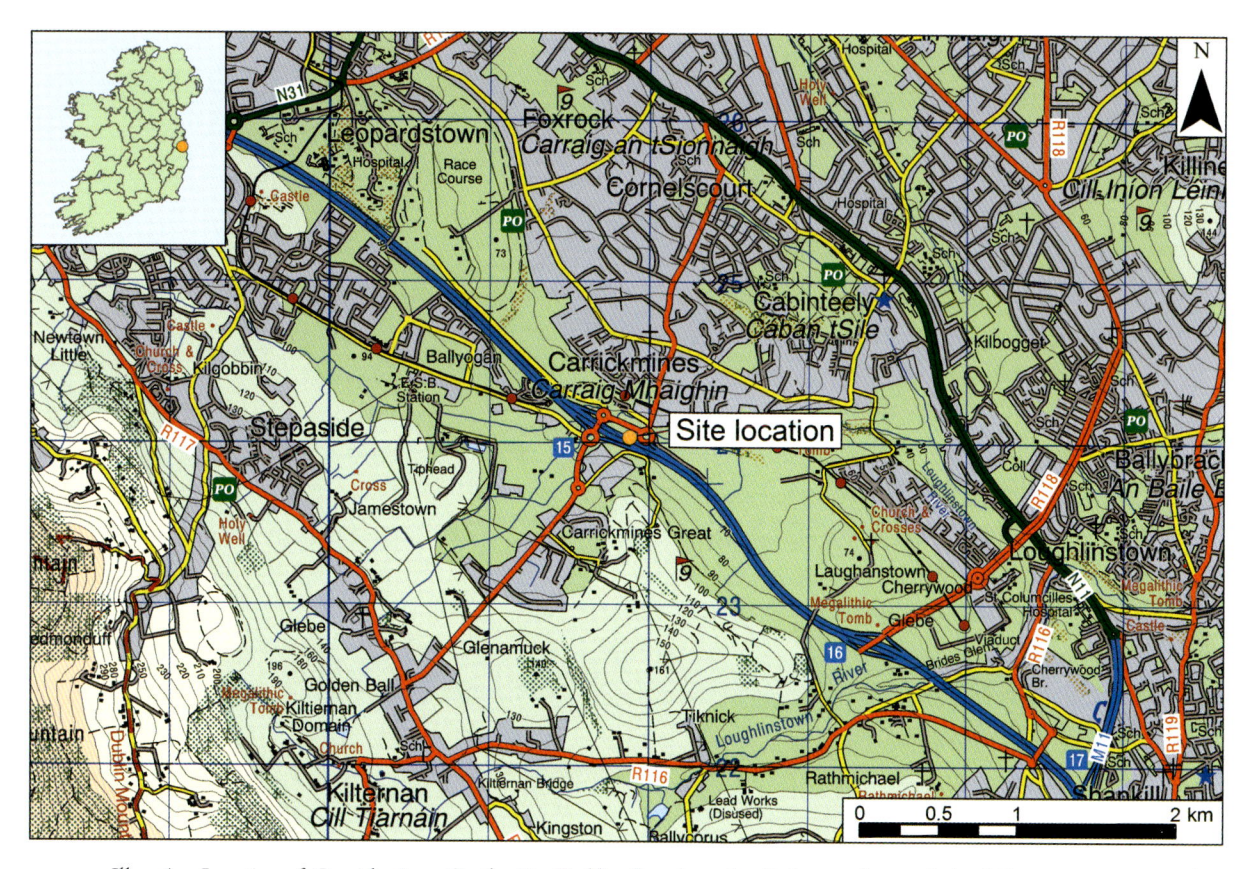

Illus. 1—Location of Carrickmines Castle, Co. Dublin (based on the Ordnance Survey Ireland Discovery Series map).

the selection of clay, which allows for use in heating, and the absence of glaze, which removes the danger of lead poisoning caused by lead in the glaze leaching out into food and beverages. The vessels were fired in clamp or bonfire kilns, with the result that there are no traces of a standing structure for archaeological investigation. There are a variety of vessel forms, including cooking jars, cisterns or bunghole jars, jugs, handled jars or pitchers, handled bowls, incurved dishes, dripping dishes, platters and lamps. Any decoration present is primarily on the rims and handles and occasionally on the body. Some of the decoration mirrors the applied pads on glazed wares, made with a small ball of clay pressed onto the surface of the body. A repeated decoration on the cooking jars appears to have been made with a fragment of cockleshell impressed into the body.

Leinster Cooking Ware from the national roads excavations

The many large-scale urban and rural excavations in recent years have contributed greatly to our knowledge of the materials used in the medieval period. As pottery of the 12th–14th century was used widely by the Anglo-Normans, it provides a point of comparison between urban and rural sites. The road scheme excavations carried out under the auspices of the NRA, particularly in the south-east, provide the principal focus of this paper, with highlighted defended farmstead sites from townlands with evocative names: Ballykeoghan, Earlsrath and Leggetsrath East (N9/N10 Kilcullen–Waterford) in County Kilkenny; and Moneycross Upper (N11 Gorey–Arklow Link), Ballydawmore (M11 Gorey–Enniscorthy), Landscape (N25 New Ross Bypass) and Coolamurry (N30 Clonroche–Enniscorthy) in County Wexford.[2]

The material from these sites can be set against the quantity and range of Leinster Cooking Ware found at Carrickmines Castle (Illus. 2 & 3), where over 75% of the almost 50,000 sherds is of Leinster Cooking Ware. Other sites in the south of Dublin, such as at Nangor Castle, Dundrum Castle and Merrion Castle, have yielded a range of 40–99% of Leinster Cooking Ware and these four castle sites, all within a radius of c. 8 km, would have provided excellent markets for the local production of Leinster Cooking Ware. These sites are essentially larger versions of the defended farmsteads listed above, but the bigger the settlement, the more necessary is the support group to run it. The inhabitants of such sites were more likely to have used the cheaper, more easily obtainable wares that may have been accessible on a local basis or even produced under the patronage of one of the centres, while the slightly more difficult to acquire items made in the city or purchased with the wine from overseas would have been used only by the people at the top of the social pyramid. Leinster Cooking Ware might be said to be traditionally associated with low-status occupation, but this has the effect of devaluing materials or vessels that have been the choice of a considerable number of people over a long period of time. The carelessly chosen term 'a simple pulled spout', for example, misunderstands the complexity of the potters' craft, however lowly that craft may have been viewed both by contemporaries and by later researchers. There is nothing simple about a pulled spout, as a poorly manipulated rim can be cracked or badly distorted if it is not carefully carried out. In contrast, the applied spouts, so characteristic of imported and locally made glazed jugs, allow for other defects—a poorly applied spout, or one with an inadequate pouring hole cut out, can result in a jug that actually functions less well than that without a spout or with a 'simple' pulled spout.

---

[2] Ballykeoghan: NGR 257879, 119825; height 27 m OD; Excavation Licence No. E2502; Ministerial Direction No. A032; Excavation Director Graeme Laidlaw.
 Earlsrath (Site AR033): NGR 256319, 127209; height 117 m OD; Excavation Reg. No. E3007; Ministerial Direction No. A032; Excavation Director Liam McKinstry.
 Leggetsrath East: NGR 253793, 156484; height 54 m OD; Excavation Licence No. E3734; Ministerial Direction No. A032; Excavation Director Emma Devine.
 Moneycross Upper (Site 6): NGR 312629 155715; height 40 m OD; Excavation Licence Reg. E3471; Ministerial Direction No. A003; Excavation Director Holger Schweitzer.
 Ballydawmore 4: NGR 301262 141455; height 48 m OD; Excavation Reg. No. E4278; Ministerial Direction No. A054; Excavation Director Colum Hardy.
 Landscape 2: NGR 270868, 123906; height 260 m OD; Excavation Reg. No. E4108; Ministerial Direction No. A052; Excavation Director James Hession.
 Coolamurry (Site 4): NGR 291382, 137239; height 100 m OD; Excavation Licence No. 04E0326; Excavation Director Grace Fegan.

In praise of Leinster Cooking Ware

Illus. 2—Aerial view of Carrickmines Castle and the Glenamuck Road (top left) c. 1960, showing what is traditionally believed to be part of a gatehouse. By 1781 this was the only upstanding part of the castle buildings (photographer unknown, courtesy of Valerie J Keeley Ltd).

Illus. 3—Aerial view of Carrickmines Castle during excavation, showing the rectangular bawn (defended enclosure) surrounded by three ditches. The post-1800 Glenamuck Road crosses the site and the farm buildings are on the left (Valerie J Keeley Ltd).

It is worth adding here part of the definition given in the Medieval Pottery Research Group (1998) classification of medieval ceramic forms to be clearer:

'The jar form is frequently called a Cooking Pot, a term which has a specific functional implication. While it is undoubtedly true that many of these vessels were used for cooking, a simple utilitarian form might also have been used for a multitude of other functions, which could have changed during the life of the vessel. The term Jar, therefore, is recommended in order to avoid possibly spurious functional connotation and the term Cooking Pot should be used only for vessels that show evidence for cooking in the form of sooting and burnt residues.'

It is always tempting to judge archaeological materials in the light of current fashions and trends. Even the rapid changes of the last 10 years that have led to the purchase of ready-made meals over home-cooked meals has diminished our ability to see the potential for many vessels. For example, what is the use of a dripping dish to catch the fats and meat juices for potential gravy if you are of a generation that thinks making gravy consists only of a powder mixed with boiling water!

While the majority of vessels in Leinster Cooking Ware are the jar used primarily for cooking, based on the burning and soot build-up found on the exterior, three illustrations from the Carrickmines excavations cover some of the other, more interesting vessels.

Bunghole jars or cisterns

These vessels start out as a rounded jar form, very similar in shape to the cooking pots. It is the addition of the component part (i.e. the bunghole) that identifies the function of this particular jar—although the profile of the vessel is identical to the vessel commonly referred to as a cooking pot. It is rare to recover a vessel with a complete profile, but one example from Carrickmines Castle allows for some comment (Illus. 4). It may be that the softly flaring rim is characteristic of those jars modified as bunghole jars or cisterns. It would be foolhardy to make such a definite claim, however, based on a single example, and it would be wiser to suggest only that the two may be found together. Given these defining characteristics, these vessels should therefore be described as rounded bunghole jars or cisterns. The bunghole in jars or cisterns of Leinster Cooking Ware typically appears to be a perforated circular knob or disc of clay applied to the exterior of the vessel wall. These vessels were used to hold water and ale, among other liquids, with the sediments sitting below the lowest part of the bunghole. Some 16 of these vessels are represented in the pottery remains recovered at Carrickmines, while a further 14 were found at the Merrion Castle site. It was clearly a popular vessel in the south Dublin area.

Dripping dishes and platters

These are recognisable from their thickness, characteristic sand-marked underside and smooth surface. Vessels of this type were often made as flat slabs, similar to an oval

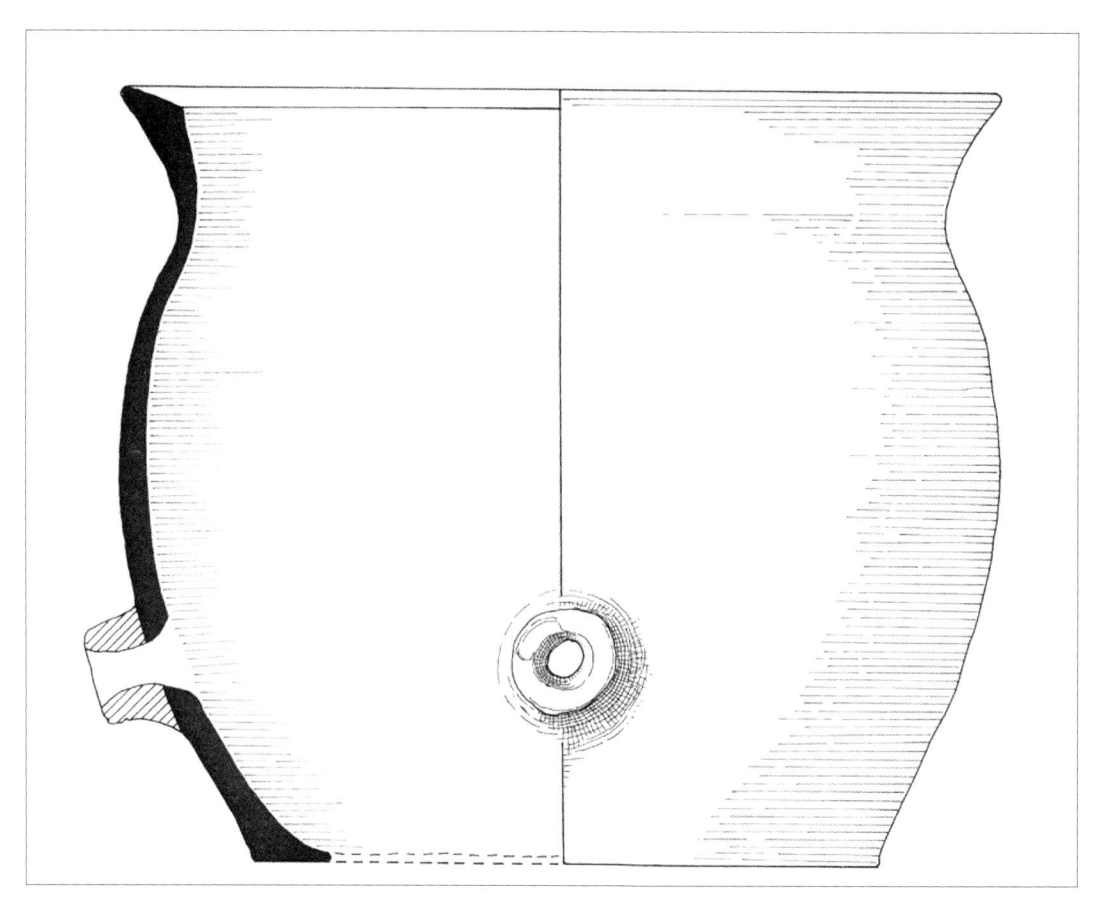

Illus. 4—Leinster Cooking Ware bunghole jar (Find No. 00E0525:2/1120; not to scale) from Carrickmines Castle (Rhoda Cronin-Allanic).

bread board, but examples with low edges are also known (Illus. 5). A considerable number were found in the 1980s during excavations at Jerpointchurch and Kilferagh, both in County Kilkenny, and more recently at all of the NRA road scheme sites listed above. It may be that these are a particular favourite in the south-east (i.e. Wexford and Kilkenny).

Lamps

Leinster Cooking Ware lamps were made as single cressets, based on a stone prototype. There is no distinguishable stem, but a gentle flaring at the bottom and top. They would have been very easy to carry, grasped around the waist of the lamp. A cup at the top would probably have held the oil and the wick, but the lamp fragments found to date show only a hollowed area through the centre, more likely to assist in firing by reducing the thickness of the stem. Sherds from Leinster Cooking Ware lamps are often only recognisable by the smooth outer surface and by the very low-fired, crumbly inner material. Indistinguishable sherds, almost prehistoric in appearance, are often the only surviving remains. Lamp fragments were found at Coolamurry 4 and

Landscape 2, Co. Wexford, on the NRA road scheme excavations, with others derived from excavations in Waterford City and Ferns Castle, Duncormick, Bricketstown and Bridgetown Lower, all in County Wexford, the latter with the hint of a cup-shaped top.

Jugs

In all of the sites mentioned in this paper, one or more jugs were recovered. None is very big, with the average vessel holding about two pints of liquid. The handles are generally strap shaped with a variety of stabbed and slashed decoration, all very much less regular than that seen on the contemporary glazed jugs. A pinched decoration

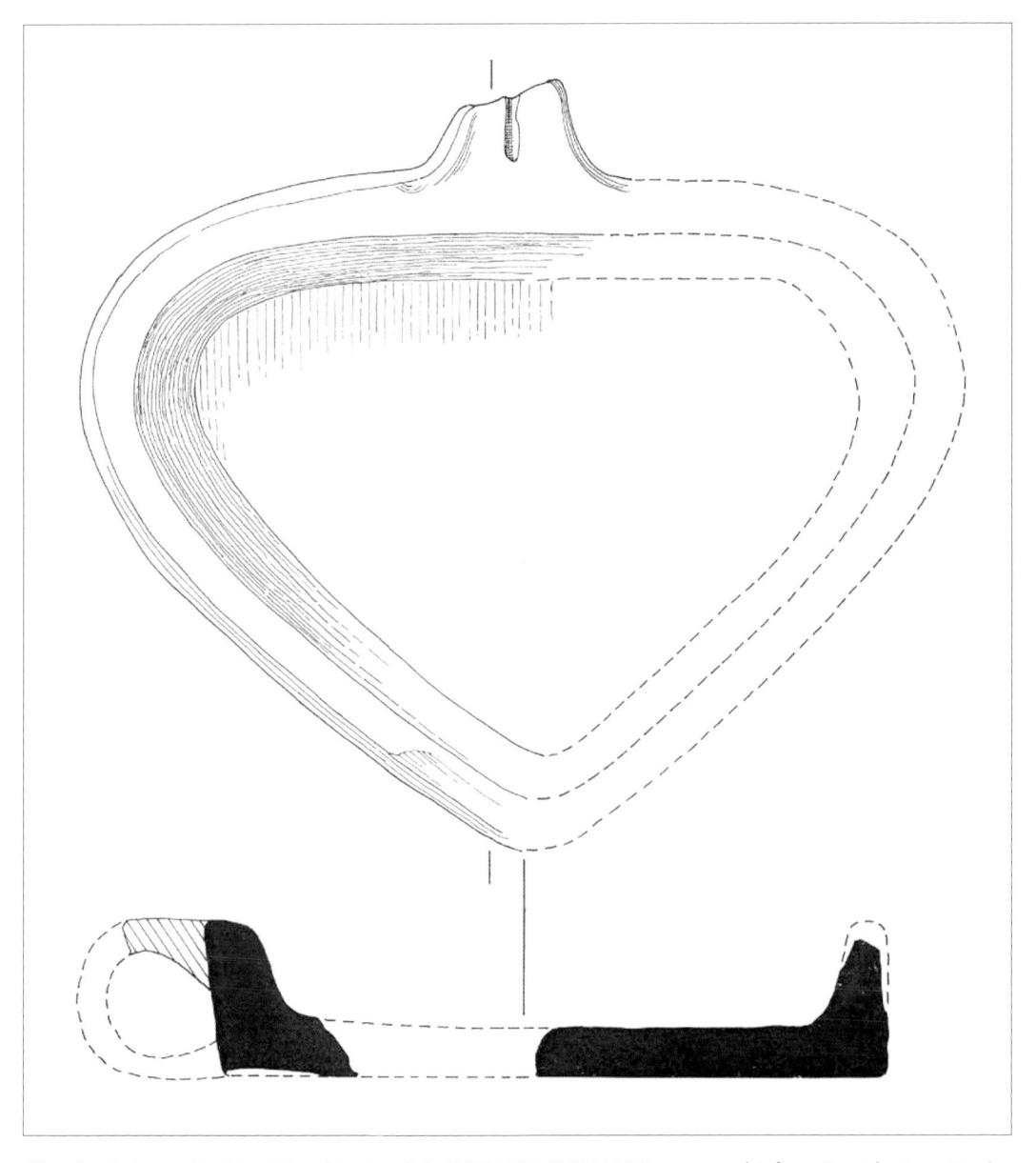

Illus. 5—Leinster Cooking Ware dripping dish (00E0525:847/1794; not to scale) from Carrickmines Castle (Rhoda Cronin-Allanic).

often occurs around the rim and both decorative treatments are present on the illustrated jug from Carrickmines (Illus. 6), where the remains of at least 46 jugs were present. This vessel has a rounded belly and a slight curve on the base, possibly to set into a dip in a mud floor.

Conclusions

The NRA-funded excavations on the Wexford/Kilkenny road schemes discussed were, by and large, at the sites of defended farmsteads. It is tempting to paint the picture of a comfortable and prosperous farming family, trading within the local

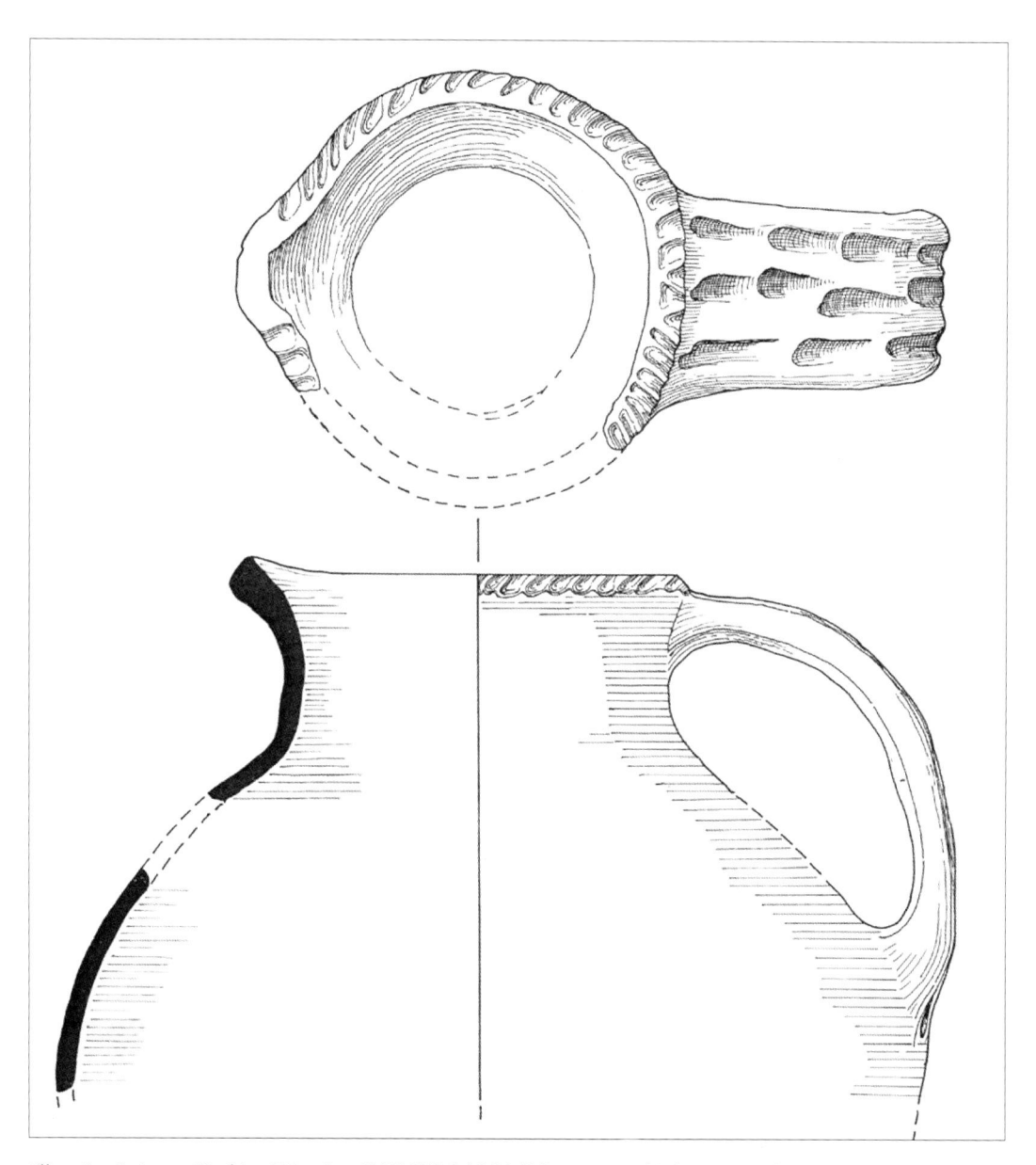

Illus. 6—Leinster Cooking Ware jug (00E0525:1980/32; not to scale) from Carrickmines Castle (Rhoda Cronin-Allanic).

area and using some unglazed vessels on the table, along with wooden and metal containers. Leinster Cooking Ware, with its variety of vessels, was an integral part of the home and although there might have been an issue with the gritty surfaces, the lack of potentially poisonous lead glaze was a further bonus. There may have been individual wooden plates, with food served from a large cooking pot that had been set on the hearth fire; the roast placed on a dripping dish to catch the juices, with dessert set out on a platter; the table lit by an oil lamp; ale or wine or even fresh water drawn from a pottery cistern set in the corner and brought to the table in a decorated pottery jug, poured out into wooden drinking cups; each person with their own knife, usually carried on the person, and wooden or bone spoons. Happy homesteads indeed!

Acknowledgements

My thanks to the NRA for the invitation to present this material to the 2013 annual seminar and to Rhoda (Cronin) Allanic for her wonderful pottery illustrations.

9. Witnesses to history: a military assemblage from the 1691 Aughrim battlefield

Damian Shiels

The techniques of conflict and battlefield archaeology are increasingly being employed as a means of revealing new information about violent encounters in the past. Methodologies based around battlefield investigation have been developed over the past 30 years and are now widely employed on sites across the United States of America, the United Kingdom and mainland Europe. The principal tool used by battlefield archaeologists is the systematic, controlled collection of artefacts from a conflict site using metal-detection. The results have had a dramatic impact on our understanding of some of the most highly traumatic events in human history. This ranges from the discovery of weapons and equipment dropped by Roman soldiers wiped out by German tribesmen at Kalkriese in AD 9 to tracking the individual bullet signatures of doomed members of the 7th U.S. Cavalry on the 1876 Little Bighorn battlefield in Montana. Viewed in their context, objects from sites, which might individually be regarded as unremarkable, have the potential to reveal poignant information about individuals who found themselves in the maelstrom of battle.

Although still in its infancy on the island of Ireland, recent years have witnessed a growth in the application of battlefield archaeology methodologies. Conflict sites such as the Yellow Ford, Co. Armagh (1598), Kinsale, Co. Cork (1601), and the Boyne, counties Meath and Louth (1690), have all revealed artefactual evidence for the engagements that occurred there. This paper will focus on a small but important assemblage of objects recovered from the 1691 battlefield of Aughrim, Co. Galway, during archaeological works in advance of the construction of the M6 Galway–Ballinasloe motorway (Illus. 1).

The Battle of Aughrim

On 12 July 1691 the tranquillity of east County Galway was shattered when some 40,000 men moved into the fields and hills around the village of Aughrim. What followed was one of the bloodiest encounters in Irish history; by 13 July thousands of men lay dead, scattered across the countryside. The memory of the Battle of Aughrim has remained strong in Ireland, with dozens of poems and laments testifying to its significance in Irish consciousness. These references began shortly after the defeat and have continued into modern times; as recently as 1968 poet Richard Murphy produced a major oratorio entitled 'The Battle of Aughrim' (Simms 1977).

The battle forms part of what is known in Ireland as the 'War of the Two Kings' (*Cogadh an Dá Rí*), namely the deposed James II and the reigning King William III. During the winter of 1690–1 the Jacobites (those fighting to restore James as King)

Fragments of Lives Past

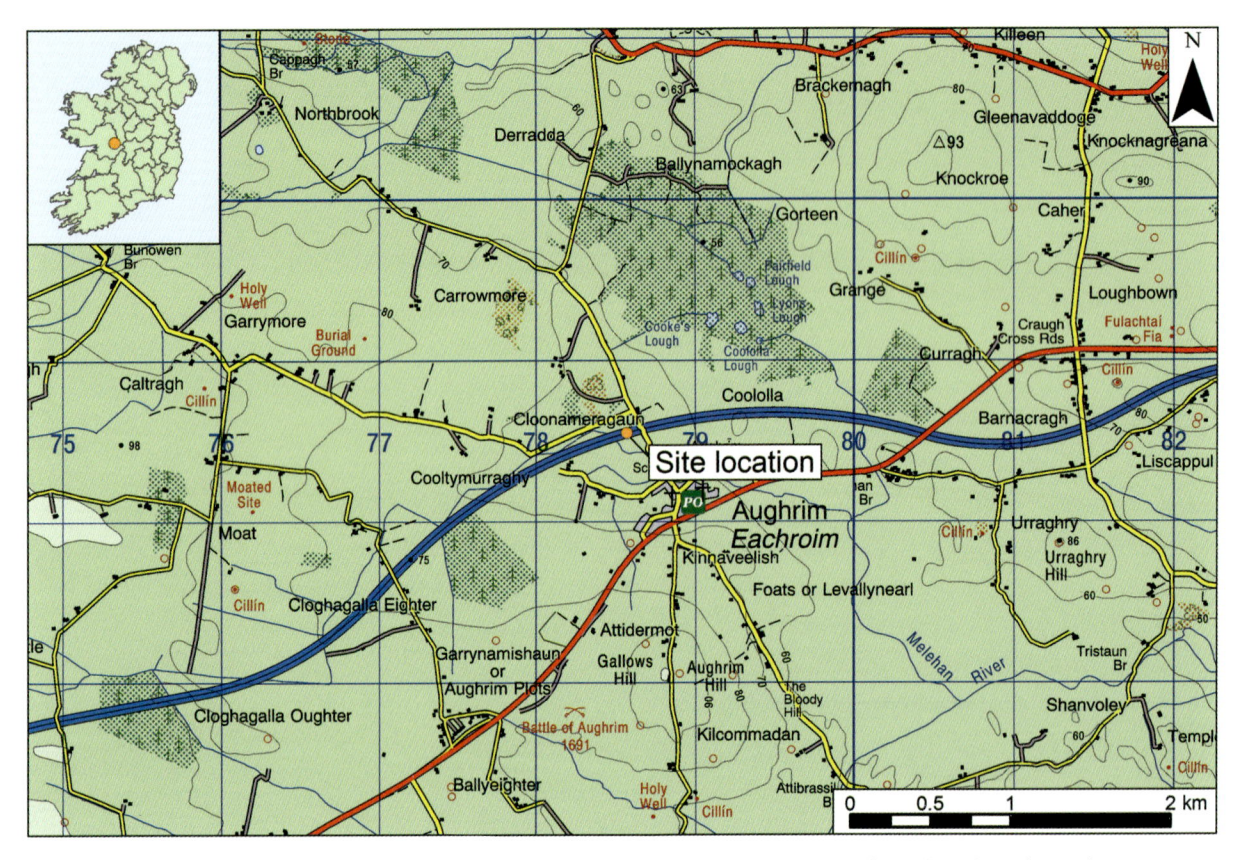

Illus. 1—Location of Luttrell's Pass metal-detection survey near Aughrim, Co. Galway (based on the Ordnance Survey Ireland Discovery Series map).

held a line along the River Shannon, garrisoning key strong points, such as Athlone and Limerick. The fall of Athlone on 30 June 1691 allowed the Williamite army, under the command of the Dutchman Godert de Ginkel, to cross the Shannon in force. The Jacobite commander, the Frenchman Charles Chalmont, Marquis de St Ruth, pulled back in the face of their advance, moving to place his army on good ground, where they could make a stand and block the Williamite approach. The stage was set for the Battle of Aughrim.

St Ruth decided to centre his army on the high ground of Kilcommodan Hill, to the south of the village of Aughrim; he commanded 14,000 infantry, 2,500 cavalry and 3,500 dragoons (mounted infantry) (Childs 2007, 332). His left flank extended to include the village and Aughrim Castle (a medieval tower house), while his right rested on the Tristaun Stream. It was a strong defensive position. Immediately to his front was a large area of boggy ground that would be difficult for the Williamite forces to cross. The likely avenues for attack were reduced to a causeway on the Jacobite left (near what is now a roadway into the village) and in the vicinity of the Tristaun Bridge, on the right. The Williamites advanced towards these Jacobite positions with 14,000 infantry, 4,000 cavalry and 2,000 dragoons, taking up positions on Urraghry Hill to the east of the Jacobites (ibid., 332). The battle began in earnest in the late morning, when Ginkel tried to drive back Jacobite outposts positioned beyond Tristaun Bridge, which after some hard fighting he succeeded in doing. A pause in the fighting ensued and the Williamites considered postponing the battle until the following day. However, they perceived that St Ruth had weakened the centre of his line (and possibly his left) by redeploying troops to support the fighting on the Jacobite right and thus determined to try and cross the boggy ground in front of the Jacobite centre to take advantage of this.

The Williamites first renewed their attack at the Tristaun Stream in an effort to pin down the Jacobite troops already positioned there. They succeeded in advancing across the stream and moved to their right, where the attack stalled amid heavy fighting at a location afterwards known as the Bloody Hollow. Meanwhile, Williamite infantry began to advance across the boggy ground towards the Jacobite centre. These soldiers found themselves wading up to their waists in water as they proceeded towards Kilcommodan Hill, but eventually they drove the first line of Jacobite defenders from the ditches closest to the boggy ground in the centre. However, the Jacobites had cut gaps in these ditches to allow for their infantry and cavalry to manoeuvre in the enclosed landscape, and they pushed the Williamites back through the bog. Hard fighting continued for a time in this area, but the Williamites were unable to make ground.

They next decided to attack along the causeway on the Jacobite left, which was defended by troops around Aughrim Castle. Williamite infantry successfully advanced up to a ditch below the castle, and they were followed by cavalry, which were only able to advance two abreast on the narrow causeway. At this moment St Ruth began to move towards this latest area of fighting, only to be decapitated by a Williamite cannonball. This was the turning-point: with his death, the Jacobites lost cohesion and central command disintegrated. Henry Luttrell, commanding the cavalry supporting the troops at Aughrim Castle, elected to lead his cavalry from the field rather than launch a sustained counter-attack against the Williamites there.

As the position collapsed, the Williamites renewed their attack in the centre and began to drive the Jacobites back. As the left and centre of the line began to be rolled up, the Jacobite right put up strong resistance, but were also eventually forced to retreat. As Jacobite troops fled from the field, many of the infantry attempted to make for the safety of a large bog to the north and west of their original position on Kilcommodan Hill, to avoid the Williamite cavalry, which was now employed in killing as many as possible of the fleeing troops. The Battle of Aughrim was over; as night fell, up to 4,000 men lay dead, their bodies scattered throughout the countryside.

Battlefield investigations

The battlefield of Aughrim is undoubtedly one of the most promising sites for the archaeological study of conflict in Ireland. It already has a large number of battle-related objects associated with it, housed in the Battle of Aughrim Interpretive Centre and in the National Museum of Ireland. Although the analytical value of this material is reduced owing to the fact that their exact findspots were not securely recorded, they nonetheless indicate that there is a large amount of surviving material relating to the battle in the fields around the village. In addition, archaeologist Natasha Ferguson investigated the site as an archaeological landscape in 2006, further highlighting its potential and revealing, through geophysical survey, the possible site of a mass grave on Kilcommodan Hill (Ferguson 2006).

In 2005 a metal-detection survey was carried out near Aughrim by Archaeological Surveys Ltd for Galway County Council and the NRA. The survey centred on 1.5 ha within the townland of Coololla, identified as the supposed location of 'Luttrell's Pass' (Record of Monuments and Places No. GA087-054), where Henry Luttrell and his cavalry were stationed behind Aughrim Castle (Illus. 2).[1] The first-edition Ordnance Survey six-inch map shows the 'Pass' as a laneway leading north-west from the castle, but the laneway is no longer extant in the modern landscape. A total of 178 objects were recovered during the survey (Sabin & Donaldson 2005, 1). Analysis of this material was carried out by Headland Archaeology (Ireland) Ltd (now trading as Rubicon Heritage Services Ltd), to determine if any of the material was related to the battle and, if so, what could be learned from it.

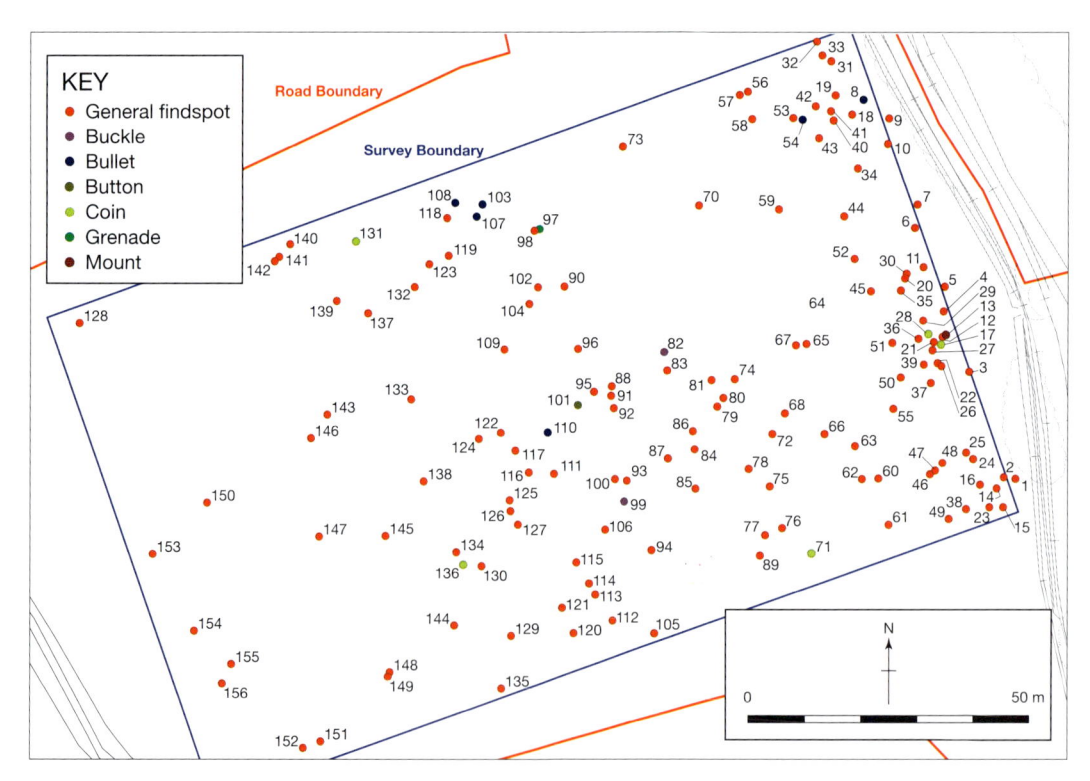

Illus. 2—All metal-detector findspots in Luttrell's Pass metal-detection survey (after Sabin & Donaldson 2005).

---

[1] NGR 178731, 2285518; height 90 m OD; Metal Detection Reg. No. R002.

Illus. 3—The grenade fragment (Find No. R002:97) and lead shot recovered from Luttrell's Pass on the Aughrim Battlefield (Rubicon Heritage Services Ltd).

A number of finds recovered during the survey were almost certainly deposited on 12 July 1691. These include seven lead bullets, a probable grenade fragment and up to four contemporary coins (Illus. 3–5). Additional items, such as a buckle (Illus. 6) and a lead badge, may also date from the battle. Analysis of the lead bullets revealed that the majority had been fired. They were weighed and measured to determine the most likely weapon of origin based on what is known of late 17th-century firearms. The bullets indicated that weapons such as pistols and carbines (a firearm shorter and lighter than a musket, used by light troops) appeared to dominate the assemblage. Both of these weapons were carried principally by mounted troops, be they cavalry or dragoons. In addition, a fragment of a metal sphere was identified as a probable hand-grenade fragment. Grenades at this time were round and hollow, the interior being filled with powder. They were carried by special troops called grenadiers, who used them by lighting a fuse at the top of the bombs and throwing them at the enemy. They were notoriously dangerous and in open field conditions could often cause injuries to friends as well as enemies. As for the coinage, though heavily corroded, one was positively identified as a copper gun-money shilling dating to 1689, with three further possible gun-money coins in the assemblage. Gun money was base metal coinage issued by the Jacobites during the course of the conflict.

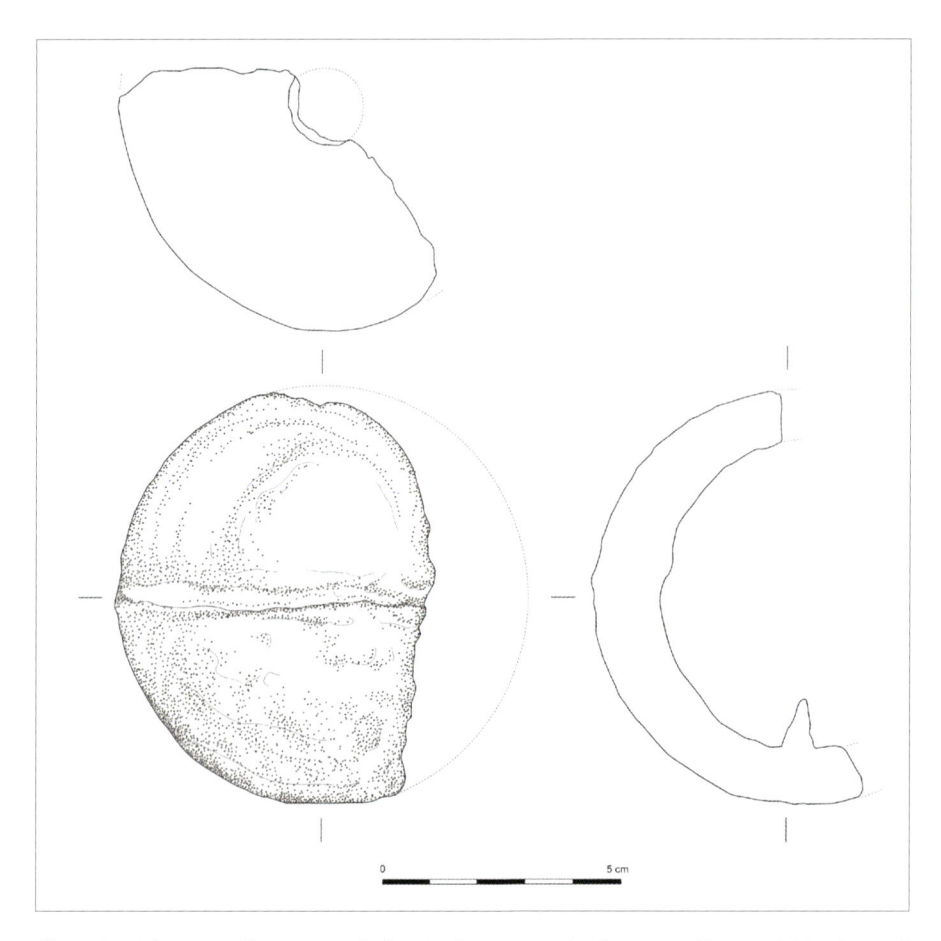

Illus. 4—Schematic illustration of the Aughrim grenade fragment (Eavan O'Dochartaigh, Rubicon Heritage Services Ltd).

Illus. 5—James II 1689 gun-money shilling (R002:21) from Luttrell's Pass (Rubicon Heritage Services Ltd).

Illus. 6—The 17th-century shoe buckle (R002:99) from Luttrell's Pass (Rubicon Heritage Services Ltd).

How can this small number of battle-related objects inform us about what happened in these fields in 1691? To discover this, it is necessary to review the primary accounts of the battle in combination with the results of the analysis. The archaeological material was recovered in a position that was to the left and rear of the Jacobite line throughout much of the fighting, and traditionally the location of a large amount of Jacobite cavalry. The front line in this sector consisted of troops stationed in and around Aughrim Castle, which covered the causeway where the Williamites eventually broke through. The Reverend George Story is perhaps the best-known chronicler of the war; he travelled with the Williamite army for much of the campaign, leaving a record of events as he saw them. He described the ferocious fighting along the causeway and at Aughrim Castle, which eventually led to the forcing of the causeway. As the Jacobite left began to disintegrate, he states:

> 'So that notwithstanding all their advantages of Hedges and Ground, Sun and Wind, they were forced to quit one advantageous Post, and after that another, till being beat from Ditch to Ditch, they were driven up to the Top of the Hill of Kilkommodon, where their Camp had laid, which being levelled, and they exposed to our Shot more openly, they began now to run down right; the Foot towards a great Bogg behind them on their left, and the Horse on the Highway towards Loughreagh . . . ' (Story 1693, 134)

Despite this initial Jacobite collapse towards the left and centre, the men on the right continued to fight on for a considerable time. When they eventually broke, the Jacobites 'fled all out of the Field; their Foot were miserably slaughtered by our Horse and Dragoons, as they made towards the Bogg' (Story 1693, 134–5) (Illus. 7). Captain Robert Parker was another Williamite commentator present at the battle. He describes how the Williamite horse 'made a great slaughter of their Foot in the pursuit, which we continued till night came on' (Parker 1746, 31).

Following the clearing of the battlefield the Williamite forces would have settled down to strip the bodies of all valuables, including their clothing. This activity probably took place during dusk or after night had fallen. Story described the post-battle scene:

> '. . . looking amongst the Dead three days after, when all our own and some of theirs were buried, I reckoned in some small Inclosures 150 in others 120 &c. lying most of them by the Ditches where they were Shot; and the rest from the top of the Hill where their Camp had been, looked like a great Flock of Sheep, shattered up and down the Countrey, for almost four miles round . . .' (Story 1693, 137)

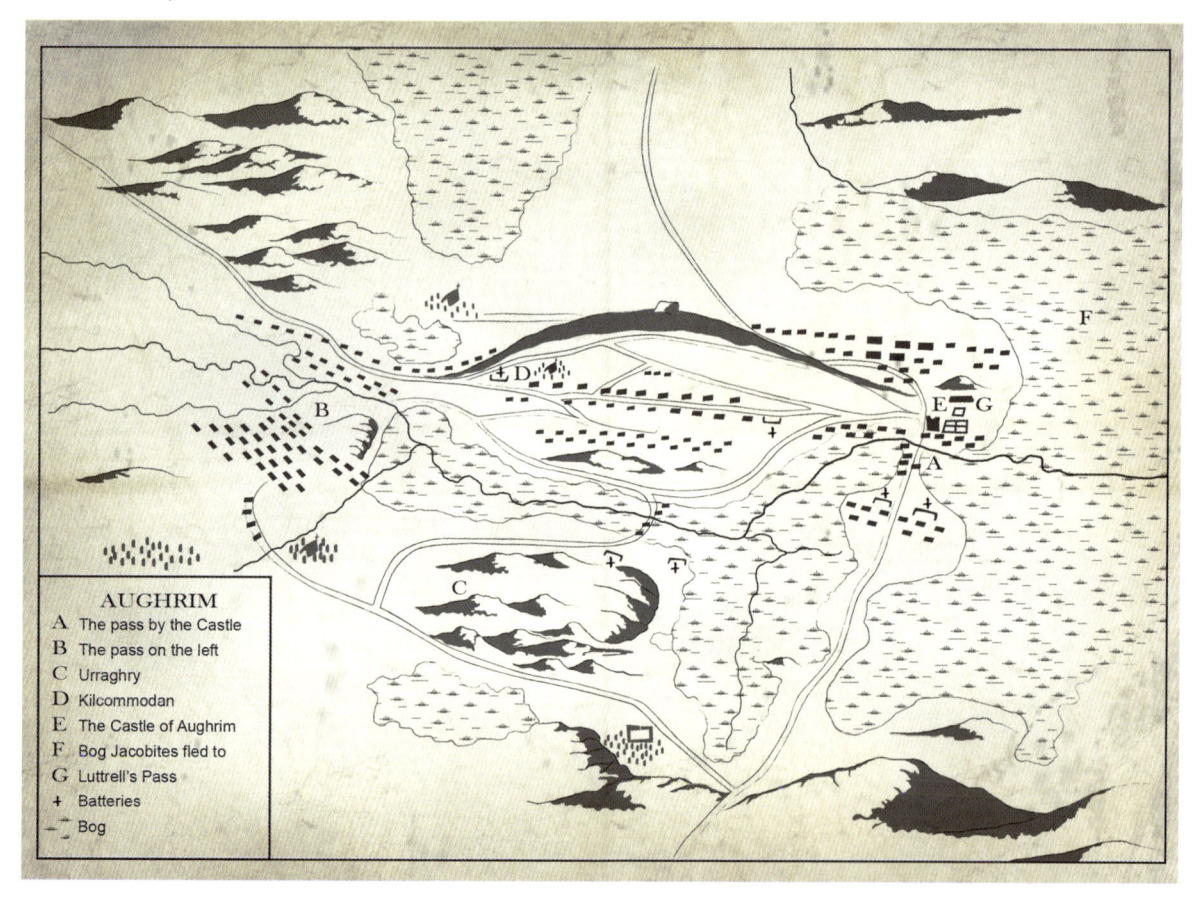

Illus. 7—Adaptation of the Reverend George Story's map of the Battle of Aughrim, with letters and text adapted for ease of reference. The bog to which the Jacobites fled is the one marked 'F' in the upper right quadrant. The position of the various troop formations is indicated by rectangular blocks (Jonathan Millar, Rubicon Heritage Services Ltd, after Story 1693).

These accounts give us two key pieces of information. First, we know that when the Jacobite lines broke, many of the infantry attempted to escape the Williamite cavalry and dragoons by running for a large bog located to the left and rear of the Jacobite positions, behind where Luttrell's Pass is currently located. Secondly, we know that the Williamites stripped the bodies of the dead Jacobites to retrieve valuables: that they were naked is attested by Story's reference to their appearing like 'a great Flock of Sheep', owing to the pale skin of the fallen.

The location of the metal-detection survey and the small number of military artefacts recovered make it clear that this position was not a scene of intense fighting during the battle. It may well have been the location of some of Luttrell's cavalry, but as they do not appear to have been heavily engaged here before retreating, they would have left behind little in the way of artefacts. What we can say with some degree of confidence is that there was fighting in this field. Although the fired bullets may have travelled some distance before being deposited in the ground, it is probable that a number were discharged at a downward angle close to their eventual findspot. The presence of the probable exploded hand grenade (Illus. 4 & 5) confirms that infantry traversed the field on the day of the battle. With this and the historical information, it is possible to suggest an interpretation of this small military assemblage, based on an analysis of the objects in conjunction with the contemporary sources. Let us imagine for a moment a possible scenario.

A soldier's tale

It's late in the day and the battle is lost for the Jacobites. There is nothing left for the men to do except try to save themselves. A group race away from the carnage, desperately trying to find safety. Their best hope is the bog they noticed before the battle. It shouldn't be too far away and it offers some hope of escape—at least the horses cannot follow them there. Where are the damned Jacobite cavalry? The men are defenceless without them, especially now that the Williamites are pouring their own cavalry and dragoons into the pursuit. They are closing in. One of the men risks a glance back; they are thundering after them, right on their tails. The group behind haven't made it, they hear their shouts and cries as they are cut down to a man. But there isn't far to go. Only a few hundred feet and they'll be safe, at least for now. Most of the men have thrown away their weapons and equipment to run faster, straining every muscle to get clear.

Their hearts beat like never before, as they are literally in a race for their lives. The firing moves closer and one of the group crumples and falls. The Williamite dragoons are shooting at them now. They're not going to make it. Breathless, a Jacobite grenadier decides to make a desperate stand. He turns to face the oncoming riders. Reaching for his last grenade, he fumbles to light the fuse. With his final reserves of energy he hurls it at the Williamites, who scatter as the deadly weapon wings its way towards them. He watches as the grenade explodes harmlessly, resigned to his fate. The cavalry are on him now and the end is quick. The Williamite trooper manoeuvres his mount at a fast trot to get into position, dispatching the grenadier with a single blow of his sword. He looks around for his next target.

It is now dusk and the Williamite infantry have arrived in the area. They're weary and exhausted from the terrible fighting of the day, but they are victorious. All around are the bodies of Jacobites who did not survive the rout. They lie in ones and twos across the field, but all is now quiet; the battle is over here. The campaign has been a physical drain on all of these men, but now is their opportunity for reward. They begin to search the bodies for valuables, hoping to come across an officer or person of rank. Night is falling fast and soon more men will arrive to see if there is anything to be had. They hurry to check as many bodies as they can. In the half-light they fumble through the bloodied clothes of the Jacobites, but in their haste some coins fall loose into the churned-up field. They are probably Jacobite gun money and not worth the time it would take to retrieve them; better to move on to the next body, to see if they have better luck.

Conclusion

This is one potential interpretation for the events that led to the deposition of the small military assemblage recovered at Luttrell's Pass during the archaeological works on the M6, and clearly it is conjecture. However, it does highlight just how valuable even a seemingly insignificant assemblage of battlefield objects can be if they are retrieved and recorded correctly. This material forces the observer to think about how these items were deposited and to look again for explanations in the primary accounts. Perhaps their greatest value is that they refocus our attention on the individual in a battle that involved tens of thousands, every one of whom had different and very personal experiences on that bloody day.

Acknowledgements

Thanks to Alison Kyle for providing analysis of the buckles, buttons and a decorative mount. Jonathan Millar, Eavan O'Dochartaigh, Sara Nylund and Louise Baker prepared the graphics for publication. This work was carried out as part of the archaeological works associated with the construction of the M6 Galway–Ballinasloe motorway and analysis was funded by Galway County Council and the NRA. Special thanks to NRA Archaeologist Jerry O'Sullivan for the opportunity to analyse this important assemblage.

10. Experimental archaeology: making; understanding; story-telling

Aidan O'Sullivan, Mark Powers, John Murphy, Niall Inwood, Bernard Gilhooly, Niamh Kelly, Wayne Malone, John Mulrooney, Cian Corrigan, Maeve L'Estrange, Antoinette Burke, Maria Kazuro, Conor McDermott, Graeme Warren, Brendan O'Neill, Mark Heffernan & Mairead Sweeney

Experimental archaeology can be defined as the reconstruction of buildings, technologies, objects and environmental contexts, based on archaeological evidence, in order to investigate the materiality of people's lives in the past. It can explore, through replication, the archaeological traces of past activities left in the soil (e.g. the post-holes of a house, the remains of a metal-working furnace), and can also help to interpret aspects of past technologies that have left little trace (e.g. the hafting and use of stone axes, the effects of smoke inside a building). Thus experimental archaeology can ask such questions as: how did people build, occupy and abandon houses and buildings? How did they work the soil in agriculture, make and store food, interact with their environments? How did they make and use objects from a wide range of different materials? If 'archaeology is the discipline of things' (Olsen 2013), then experimental archaeology is one valuable way of investigating how people made things and in so doing, how they made their societies.

Experimental archaeology has developed its theoretical approaches across time. At the beginnings of archaeology, in the 19th century, some antiquaries practiced a form of experimental archaeological in their testing of prehistoric tools. For example, General Pitt Rivers' excavations in Cranborne Chase, in central southern England, led him to test various primitive digging tools to see how the ditches and mounds he was excavating might have been originally made. As a discipline or a practice, however, experimental archaeology really expanded in the late 1960s and 1970s with the pioneering publications and experiments of John Coles (1973) and Peter Reynolds at Butser Ancient Farm, in Hampshire, southern England, and through the work of several other scholars in Germany and Scandinavia. Their preference for empirical testing led to experimental archaeology largely having a strong scientific, positivist approach (some definitions of experimental archaeology would have a far stronger 'scientist' flavour than the one we offer above), which is still the case among some practitioners today. In recent decades, however, there have also been some influences from post-processual archaeology—a movement in archaeological theory that emphasises the subjectivity of archaeological interpretations. This has led some archaeologists to use more experiential or phenomenological approaches, exploring what it may have been like to inhabit a building, or how past people's embodied encounters with material culture should be explored through our senses, that is through our hands, eyes, smell and hearing. In this sense, experimental archaeology can benefit by engagement with writers like the sociologist Richard Sennett, or through adopting anthropological approaches, such as those proposed by Ian Hodder and Tim Ingold, who explore how things are made, felt, heard and seen, as well as understood—how we think with our hands as well as with our heads and, most importantly, how people's lives are entangled with their environments through their understanding and use of material resources.

Irish archaeology also has a long, if patchy, tradition of experimental archaeology. This stretches back to the building of a Neolithic house at Lough Gur, Co. Limerick, by Prof. Seán P Ó Ríordáin, for a BBC TV programme in the 1950s; the experiments of Prof. Michael J O'Kelly with Bronze Age *fulachtaí fia* at Ballyvourney, Co. Cork; and, more recently, through experiments with early medieval house reconstructions by Dr Tríona Nicholl; or with Bronze Age weaponry by Dr Ronan O'Flaherty and Dr Barry Molloy at University College Dublin (UCD). In the last few years, UCD School of Archaeology has embarked on an ambitious programme of experimental archaeology research and teaching, as part of a move towards a stronger engagement with material culture studies generally. With the help of the university, we have established the UCD Centre for Experimental Archaeology and Ancient Technologies at the edge of the campus, within a fenced enclosure in an old meadow field that has become the location for a range of experimental archaeology projects that combine actual investigations with both undergraduate and graduate archaeology teaching courses. Prof. John Coles has also generously gifted his experimental archaeology archive of books, papers and unpublished materials, compiled by him since the 1960s, and we hope to digitise this collection to make it available to scholars worldwide.

In UCD, students are encouraged to design, implement and reflect on the results of their own experimental archaeology projects, presenting for assessment a portfolio of written texts, illustrations and, where appropriate, actual made objects. Among the transferable skills gained by this self-directed learning are skills in project design, resourcefulness, problem-solving, creativity and public outreach (several students have prepared podcasts or video presentations on their projects). It is also clear that there is potentially a large public interest in experimental archaeology, both on the UCD campus and beyond. In 2013 Dr Graeme Warren's project, exploring the building of a Mount Sandel-type Early Mesolithic house, was reported in national media (e.g. *The Irish Times*, RTÉ *Six One News*), as well as on various international websites devoted to archaeology (Illus. 1). UCD students have also gained expertise in presenting archaeology to the public in the last few years, through their participation in public outreach experimental archaeology demonstration events, such as during Science Week and on Dublin's Culture Night in the National Museum of Ireland; at the Institute of Archaeologists of Ireland Archaeofest event in Autumn 2013; and, of course, at the NRA annual public seminar in August 2013 (Illus. 2). Events like this are becoming more common in recent years and they allow people to engage with the past in an inclusive and meaningful way. The remainder of this paper highlights three different aspects of UCD School of Archaeology's staff and students' activities relating to stone and flint, pottery and food, as represented by UCD involvement at the NRA seminar in 2013.

Experimental archaeology: making; understanding; story-telling

Illus. 1—UCD archaeological staff and students building a Mesolithic house at the UCD Centre for Experimental Archaeology and Ancient Technologies in August 2013. Experimental archaeology projects can both interrogate aspects of the past and communicate archaeological knowledge in the present. In this case, the project was the subject of widespread TV, print and digital media interest (Aidan O'Sullivan, UCD School of Archaeology).

Illus. 2—UCD archaeological staff, Ph.D and MA scholars and undergraduate students at the NRA seminar in August 2013 (National Roads Authority).

Prehistoric stone and flint

For several years UCD staff and students have been developing their own programme focused on how prehistoric stone and flint were exploited and also their associated materials (e.g. manufactured adhesives, tendons for ties, wooden hafts). This experimental archaeology research cluster aims to replicate prehistoric stone tools, artefacts and associated ancillaries, without the use of modern implements. The purpose of the group is to informally teach (while learning ourselves) the art of tool manufacture, enabling the students to understand the raw materials, time, technologies and skills technology required. The knapping (working) of flint is the predominant activity, although grinding shale ground-stone axes is also undertaken (Illus. 3). All raw materials are sourced locally along the Irish coastline and many of the implements made are hafted in a manner that the archaeological record suggests. For example, we use a mixture of pine resin, beeswax and charcoal as an adhesive for hafting arrowheads, and binding cordage is made from tree bast (a layer of organic material between the bark and sapwood of the tree), plaited grasses, nettle stalks and animal sinew. Hammer stones used to remove flint flakes and pre-shape the implements are locally sourced, rounded beach pebbles, while soft hammers used to finish the tools consist of red deer antler billets and antler tines for pressure-flaking.

Flint-knapping is a skilled process that takes time to learn, with many moments of frustration and more than occasional bloodied fingers and hands. Flint is a sedimentary rock that fractures reasonably predictably, producing very sharp edges, hence its importance in the Mesolithic (c. 8000–4000 BC) and Neolithic (c. 4000–2400 BC) periods (before the discovery of metal, though it is used through later prehistory and occasionally into the historic periods) for a wide range of tools, such as knife blades, borers, axes, scrapers, arrowheads and denticulates (saws). Traditionally, academic publications on Mesolithic and Neolithic flint assemblages attempt to demonstrate the correct angles to strike a nodule of flint (core) with a hammer stone to remove a flake, which can then be modified to produce a tool. These publications are occasionally in error, however, and in any case, prehistoric people would have known nothing about geometry; thus we find the best way to learn is by trial and error, after being shown the basic techniques. Finishing of the implement is undertaken by soft-hammer removal of smaller flakes, and by pressure-flaking the flint surface in a 'down and outwards' motion with the end of an antler tine.

The manufacture of stone axe-heads from shale is a much simpler process to learn than knapping, although it takes a variable amount of time to produce a finished tool. A large proportion of stone axe-heads in Ireland are made of shale, which is a densely compacted mudstone. Flat, rounded, axe-shaped shale pebbles can be found on many local beaches, rolled and deposited there by countless waves. To make a stone axe-head, a chosen stone is knapped with a hammer-stone to remove flakes to thin out the material, and then a blade edge is made by grinding the knapped surface on a rough stone, such as a sandstone block. As Mandal et al. (2004) have previously

Experimental archaeology: making; understanding; story-telling

Illus. 3—Experimental and experiential archaeological projects exploring the use of stone and flint, including the production of stone axes using shale cobbles (top and middle); a range of flint blades and knives hafted, in this case, in antler (middle); and members of the UCD Experimental Archaeology Technologies Group presenting at the NRA seminar (Aidan O'Sullivan, UCD School of Archaeology, UCD Experimental Archaeology Technologies Group and National Roads Authority).

demonstrated, smaller axe-heads can be made quickly, within a few hours at most. In contrast, it should be pointed out that it can take many hours to produce axe-heads from different types of stone—porcellanite, for example. It is clear, then, that stone would have been seen as a very variable raw material in the past. Shale axe-heads make a very efficient tool for cutting down trees when they are properly hafted onto a handle. The hafting process is undertaken by choosing a suitable length of wood for a handle, which then needs a hole cut through to accept the axe-head. Many hours are needed to hew, carve and whittle a haft into the proper shape.

All endeavours improve our learning experience with regard to the way in which stone tools were manufactured in prehistoric times. Some of our efforts go unrewarded by unsuccessful knapping attempts, or by broken tools (invariably, just as the tool is being finished). However, we learn from every attempt, whether it is successful or not, and we are constantly asking ourselves and each other questions about our techniques and adjusting them accordingly. For example, some of the flint raw material available in Ireland is of poor quality, with inclusions of minerals that lead it to fracture unpredictably. Thus we have learned to adjust flaking angles and avoid suspect material areas to overcome these issues. Typically, some of the questions we ponder are: is there a more efficient way to do this? How can we speed up this process? Are we using the correct tools and techniques?

The replication of stone tools teaches us, through learning and experimentation, how implements may have been manufactured and the exploitation of the resource in terms of time and skills required. This gives us an insight into the importance these items would have held in prehistory and allows us to tentatively reconstruct the tasks undertaken in this period. Along the way we have made important discoveries that could only have been realised by experimentation and replication. For example, most believe that an axe-head would be considered more valuable than its haft, although, as we have mentioned, in terms of labour expended the reverse is, in fact, the case. Shale axe-head production requires some labour, but this pales into insignificance compared to the production of the handle. First, a branch has to be cut from a tree and the bark stripped, then the wood must be hewn, carved and whittled, which are lengthy processes when using only flint and shale tools. However, it is the creation of the socket in which the axe-head resides that takes the most time. We have discovered two ways of doing this: by boring with a pointed flint awl, or by burning through the haft. The latter is best undertaken by placing a smouldering ember on the wood and re-energising it by blowing through a hollow piece of grass, which then allows the burnt wood to be scraped out. Both of these methods are extremely lengthy processes and this example shows that in the case of axes, the haft would have been more valued than the axe-head, purely because of the time expended in manufacture. Further experimentation is planned to explore how effective stone tools are, how best to use them, how often they have to be replaced or repaired and the implications of all of this for society.

Pottery

UCD archaeologists have also been exploring pottery manufacturing, focusing in particular on Bronze Age Beakers, early medieval Souterrain Ware and medieval Leinster Cooking Ware (see McCutcheon, Chapter 8), all relatively simple handmade vessels fired in open fires (Illus. 4). Bronze Age Beaker vessels are one of many forms of prehistoric pots that have survived throughout Europe. One of our experimental archaeology pottery projects has focused on an assemblage uncovered during excavations by Prof. Seán P Ó Ríordáin at Grange Stone Circle, Lough Gur, Co. Limerick. Petrological analysis of the material from the excavations has shown that a variety of inclusions were used in the manufacture of the vessels, including one sherd containing crushed bone (Cleary 1984, 73). Bone-tempered pottery raises some interesting questions regarding traditions in ceramic technology. This prompted a comparative analysis of the use of different forms of temper for pottery production.

Even in its most primitive form, the making of pottery demands five distinct processes: digging the clay; preparing it; forming the pottery; drying it; and firing it (Hodges 1989, 19). The clay for the experiment was sourced from the shoreline of the Poulaphouca Reservoir, located in the granite mountains of north-west Wicklow. The clay found there is quite malleable, being derived from the sediments of an early postglacial lake. No clay is suitable for making pottery immediately after digging: first, it must be worked into a homogenous mass and any lumps of extraneous matter or impurities must be removed (Cleary 2000, 125). The clay is pulverised with water, added to create a workable medium for bonding and forming processes. Once processed, the temper is added to the clay to improve workability. Furthermore, the temper inclusions prevent shrinking and cracking during the firing process. Crushed bone was added for the production of one vessel and coarse grain sand was added to another. The production method employed was the pinch pot method, a hand-held sculpting technique. This is quite an efficient method for creating prehistoric pots. Each vessel was left to dry naturally for five to six weeks in a dry room before firing. (It is likely that in prehistory pots would have been dried beside a domestic hearth for a few weeks.)

Early pottery was fired in open fires at temperatures of 1,000°C and is described by modern potters as *terracotta* (Hodges 1989, 24). The firing of clay not only changes its fundamental chemistry but also changes the colour of the final product. The firing technique we employed at the UCD Centre for Experimental Archaeology and Ancient Technologies was an open bonfire set in a shallow pit, known as a clamp kiln. At about 10.00am the leather-hard pottery vessels were initially placed around the perimeter of the fire for over an hour, to facilitate the removal of any excess moisture, at the end of which time the pot changes colour to a duskier hue. At this point the pot has reached the 'water-smoking' stage and is ready for full firing. The fire was allowed to die down slightly to hot embers and the pottery was placed within the core of the fire, then additional fuel was added to cover the assemblage. As the fire developed through the afternoon, we could establish, using hand-held infra-red thermometers and associated probes, that we were reaching a relatively high temperature of well over 800°C, and probably a bit above 1,000°C for extended periods. Clay is transformed

Illus. 4—Experimental archaeology firing of different types of Bronze Age and early medieval pottery at the UCD Centre for Experimental Archaeology and Ancient Technologies in April and May 2013. Archaeology students can learn about pottery technologies by digging their own clays and temper, by making various pot shapes using pinch and coil techniques, and by firing pots through the various stages required (Aidan O'Sullivan, UCD School of Archaeology).

into ceramic when heated at temperatures above 550–650°C. Our firing process proved to be effective and all pots were fired successfully, without losses. The transformation process was quite enjoyable, involving the fascination of heat and flames, a feeling of sociability around the fire, and a time of discovery as the fire was allowed to die down and the pots were removed after c. 4.00pm. The vessels were taken out using sticks, with the body of the pot measured at over 300°C, and then plunged into buckets of cold water. Bubbles and steam resulted from the sudden immersion and a deeper red colour was created on the pot's surface.

It seems likely that pottery firing was a sociable activity, but one that was also a moment of symbolic and transformative power. The firing session allowed us to envision a small community of prehistoric people congregating and telling stories around a hot fire, with glowing embers illuminating the night. Post-firing observations demonstrated that the pots were successfully transformed to ceramic and each vessel retained liquid without any leakage. However, each pot contained 'fire clouds' (black surfaces against the oxidised red-brown-coloured pot), which suggests that the oxidisation process was not complete. Perhaps this was a result of fluctuations in the fire's temperature. It is clear that prehistoric potters may have had significant control over their fire, maintaining a consistent temperature. There are further questions to be asked about firing processes: for example, an alternative method for firing could incorporate a turf-kiln superstructure. The project allowed us to appreciate the full spectrum of the processes involved in the manufacture of prehistoric pots. Moreover, such studies enable us to engage with the material and to contemplate particular challenges that may have arisen for producing such objects in the past.

Food and cooking

Some of the UCD experimental archaeology students also took on the task of food preparation to test ancient cooking methods, using ingredients both gathered and purchased, with the intent of critically analysing the end result. Using an open fire in the UCD Centre for Experimental Archaeology and Ancient Technologies to cook on, the team particularly consulted the writing of the archaeologist and ancient food writer Jacqui Wood, author of *Prehistoric Cooking* (2001) and *Tasting the Past* (2009), paying close attention to a section on clay-baking, since this was of specific interest as a form of cooking (Illus. 5).

It was decided that fish was a good raw ingredient to test, as it would not take too long to cook and would have been readily available in rivers, lakes and coastal regions in ancient times. Although fish was the main ingredient used during the course of the experiments, some ham was also used, accompanied by ingredients gathered in the wild. To complement these, different types of bread mixes were baked, to provide both a sweet and savoury accompaniment to the rest of the food. Some ingredients were purchased, such as fish, ham, hazelnuts, honey and extra coarse, stone-ground wholemeal flour. Herbs, garlic, mushrooms and berries were gathered in the wild. Two pottery vessels large enough to cook in were selected, a Late Bronze Age coarse ware pot and an early medieval Souterrain Ware pot, which had been previously made by other experimental archaeologists in UCD. Once the fire was lit, the experiment was ready to commence.

A whole sea bass was selected to 'clay bake'. Once the fish was cleaned out, some herbs were placed in the cavity, before the fish was wrapped in long grasses gathered at the site and secured with string. It was then encased in a mixture of clay and sand, which had been mixed together with water. The fish was placed in the fire and covered in embers for approximately 45 minutes before being removed, and the outer casing and grasses were then removed. The result was a delicious-tasting sea bass, which was succulent and moist.

While cooking the fish in the fire, it had been decided to cook a fish over the fire too, as an exercise in smoking and grilling. In order to do this, a frame had to be constructed. Hazel would have been ideal wood for this exercise, but we took a shortcut and used long wooden skewers, which had been soaked in water for 20 minutes. A rainbow trout was cleaned out and flattened. Skewers were threaded through the fish horizontally and vertically, while the outer extremities of the skewers were threaded in a similar manner to form a frame. The frame was placed in a slim birch branch, which had been split in order to accommodate it, and placed at an angle over the fire. After 20 minutes the fish was removed from the fire and frame. It tasted slightly smoked, but otherwise very similar to fish that has been grilled, and would be suitable for eating both hot and cold.

Two types of stew were prepared in the pottery vessels, one with smoked fish (in this case, undyed finnan haddock, fish that had been smoked using green wood and peat) and the other with ham. Wild garlic, mushrooms, herbs and water were added to the ham, while leeks, lardons of bacon, milk and chives were added to the fish. Interestingly, when placed in the fire, the liquid in the pot containing the fish came to the boil quickly, so the pot had to be moved to a cooler part of the fire to simmer rather than boil. The liquid in the pot containing the ham did not manage to reach boiling point at all, however, regardless of where it was placed in the fire, and even when a slate lid was placed on top of it. For that reason it was decided to 'slow-cook' the ham, allowing it to remain on the fire for almost two hours. The fish stew cooked in less than an hour. Both stews were very tasty indeed.

The final food experiment entailed a type of bread mix. Using extra coarse, stone-ground wholemeal flour mixed with a little water, various ingredients were added, including chopped hazelnuts, berries, honey and herbs. The different mixtures were cooked in four different ways. One type was moulded into a bread shape, another flattened into biscuit 'patties', while the third was wrapped around fist-sized stones, which had been found at a local beach, thus creating 'bread cups', which were later filled with nuts, fruit and honey. The fourth method was to cover a cleaned-out fish with the bread mix. In each case, these different types of bread/biscuit were cooked on hot, flat stones at the side of the fire.

Tending the fire was perhaps the most difficult task, owing to the heat and smoke. This chore was undertaken mainly by one person, who found it necessary to pay it almost constant attention, moving the embers around to ensure good heat distribution. The food produced was delicious, both in terms of taste and consistency. For instance,

Illus. 5—Experimental and experiential archaeological cooking at the UCD Centre for Experimental Archaeology and Ancient Technologies in spring 2013, including testing of recipes and techniques for baking and roasting fish, fish and ham stews and breads. The archaeological evidence for food is often only actually for the ingredients, rather than the dishes. We can explore how recipes might have been prepared and how foodstuffs might have been cooked (Aidan O'Sullivan, UCD School of Archaeology).

by cooking the ham for two hours in stock developed from the wild mushrooms and herbs, the meat absorbed flavours from the additions, enhancing its overall taste. Also, despite not having been able to get the water to boil in the student-made pot, the decision to make this an experiment in slow-cooking was a worthy one, since the meat was deliciously tender. Initially, the bread cups stuck to the stones and it became necessary to use an oil to prevent that from happening. Oil or animal fat would suffice; crushing nuts, for instance, could produce oil. Once the stones were oiled and covered in the mix of flour and water, they were left by the side of the fire to dry out and bake, and then the stone was removed, leaving the bread cup to be filled with whatever the cook decided on.

The bread cups were then filled with fruit, nuts and honey. Once filled, if allowed to sit for some time, the juices from the honey and fruit seeped into the cup, making it softer and more edible, but also flavouring it nicely. As well as being filled with sweet foods, it was found that the bread cups were of a good enough consistency to withstand hot food, such as the fish stew. Although some of the liquid from the stew was absorbed into the cup, there was enough time to eat the contents before the vessel became too soggy. All in all, the experiments we carried out clearly indicated the distinct possibility that the taste of food prepared in the past was every bit as good as food prepared nowadays. In other words, food in the past need not only have been sustenance, undoubtedly it was also about taste, enjoyment, sociability and culture—food feeds both the body and soul.

Conclusions

In conclusion, experimental archaeology is as much about learning as it is about scientific discovery. To design an experimental archaeology project with research questions, one must begin by learning the basic technologies and craft skills of the past, or at least come to an appreciation of them. It is certainly the case that we can never 'be' prehistoric or medieval people, who learned since childhood how to get on in the world. We can never gain their skill sets, understand fully how they understood the properties of materials, their abilities and knowledge of their sourcing, preparation and use. We can, however, approach a sense of the embodied skills and materiality of their lives, through experimentation and experiential approaches, and can move on from there to construct experimental archaeological projects to investigate particular aspects of past societies. Since the activities described above, UCD archaeologists have constructed a Mesolithic round-house, experimented with Bronze Age and early medieval copper-smelting and bronze-casting, cooked in pits, and butchered deer and wild boar using flint blades. Future plans include the construction of an early medieval round-house and a Viking Dublin Type 1 house, and the manufacture of, among other things, a domestic assemblage of wooden, leather, textile and other equipment. Above all, UCD archaeologists aim to create things, learn about them, and tell stories about their experiences.

Appendix 1—Radiocarbon dates from excavated archaeological sites described in these proceedings

Radiocarbon ages are quoted in conventional years BP (Before Present; before AD 1950), and the errors for these dates are expressed at the one-sigma (1σ) (68% probability) level of confidence. Calibrated date ranges are equivalent to the probable calendrical age of the sample material and are expressed at one-sigma and two-sigma (2σ) (95% probability) levels of confidence. The $\delta^{13}C$ value indicates the difference between the sample's $^{13}C/^{12}C$ ratio and that of a standard. It can indicate if there is contamination in the sample or processing when the value is compared to similar material.

The date obtained from the Scottish Universities Environmental Research Centre, East Kilbride (SUERC lab code), is an AMS (Accelerator Mass Spectrometry) date calibrated using the IntCal04 (Reimer et al. 2004) calibration data set and the OxCal v.3.10 (Bronk Ramsey 2005) calibration programme. The dates obtained from Beta Analytic, Florida (Beta lab code), are AMS dates calibrated using the IntCal04 calibration data set and the Talma & Vogel (1993) calibration programme.

Lab code	Site	Sample/context	Yrs BP	$\delta^{13}C$	Calibrated date ranges
Ch. 3 The people behind the pots: considering the Early Bronze Age remains from French Furze, Tully East, Co. Kildare					
SUERC-6760	French Furze, Tully East	Hazel (*Corylus*), plum-type (*Prunus spinosa*), apple-type (Pomoideae) and ash (*Fraxinus*) charcoal from uppermost fill (C159) of pit C158	3625 ± 40	-26.1‰	2040–1920 BC (1σ) 2140–1880 BC (2σ)
Ch. 6 Dress and ornament in early medieval Ireland—exploring the evidence					
Beta-246943	Castlefarm 1	Ash (*Fraxinus*) charcoal from one of the basal fills (F851) of pit F854	1240 ± 40	-24.5‰	AD 690–810 (1σ) AD 670–890 (2σ)
Ch. 7 Early medieval E ware pottery: an unassuming but enigmatic kitchen ware?					
Beta-247009	Collierstown 1	Blackthorn (*Prunus spinosa*) charcoal from fill (F67) of the Phase 2 ditch	1530 ± 40	-21.5‰	AD 450–580 (1σ) AD 420–610 (2σ)

References

Ambrosiani, K 1981 *Viking Age Combs, Comb Making and Comb Makers: in the light of finds from Birka and Ribe.* Stockholm Studies in Archaeology 2. Stockholm University, Stockholm.

Anderson, J 1880 'Notes on the contents of two Viking graves in Islay, discovered by William Campbell, Esq., Ballinaby; with notices of the burial customs of the Norse sea-kings, as recorded in the sagas and illustrated by their grave-mounds in Norway and in Scotland', *Proceedings of the Society of Antiquaries of Scotland*, Vol. 14, 51–89.

Armit, I 2008 'Irish-Scottish connections in the first millennium AD: an evaluation of the links between souterrain ware and Hebridean ceramics', *Proceedings of the Royal Irish Academy*, Vol. 108C, 1–18.

Audouze, F 2002 'Leroi-Gourhan, a Philosopher of Technique and Evolution', *Journal of Archaeological Research*, Vol. 10, No. 4, 227–306.

Barrowman, R C, Batey, C E & Morris, C D 2007 *Excavations at Tintagel Castle, Cornwall, 1990–1999.* Society of Antiquaries, London.

Bermingham, N 2013 'Medieval settlement, industry and economy', *in* N Bermingham, F Coyne, G Hull, F Reilly & K Taylor, *River Road: the archaeology of the Limerick Southern Ring Road*, 83–114. NRA Scheme Monographs 14. National Roads Authority, Dublin.

Bland, R & Johns, C 1995 *The Hoxne Treasure: an illustrated introduction.* British Museum Publications, London.

Bøe, J 1940 'Part 3: Norse Antiquities in Ireland', *in* H Shetelig (ed.), *Viking Antiquities in Great Britain and Ireland*, 73–4. H. Aschehoug & Co., Oslo.

Bradley, J 1994–5 'Excavations at Moynagh Lough, Co. Meath', *Ríocht na Mídhe*, Vol. 9, No. 1, 158–69.

Bradley, R 2005 *Ritual and Domestic Life in Prehistoric Europe.* Routledge, London.

Breen, T 2013 *South-Eastern Motorway Scheme: Archaeological Resolution. Final report: 00E0525, 02E1532 – Carrickmines Great, County Dublin.* Unpublished report by Valerie J Keeley Ltd for Dún Laoghaire-Rathdown County Council and the National Roads Authority.

Brindley, A L 2007 *The Dating of Food Vessels and Urns in Ireland.* Bronze Age Studies 7. Department of Archaeology, NUI Galway, Galway.

Bronk Ramsey, C 2005 *OxCal Program v.3.10* (http://www.rlaha.ox.ac.uk/O/oxcal.php).

Brück, J 2006 'Ritual and rationality: some problems of interpretation in European archaeology', *in* T Insoll (ed.), *Reader in the Archaeology of Identities*, 281–306. Routledge, London.

Campbell, E 2007 *Continental and Mediterranean imports to Atlantic Britain and Ireland, AD 400–800.* CBA Research Report 157. Council for British Archaeology, York.

Carroll, J 2001 'Glass Bangles as a Regional Development in Early Medieval Ireland', *in* M Redknap, N Edwards, S Youngs, A Lane & J Knight (eds), *Pattern and Purpose in Insular Art. Proceedings of the Fourth International Conference on Insular Art held at the National Museum & Gallery, Cardiff 3–6 September 1998*, 101–14. Oxbow, Oxford.

Case, H 1961 'Irish Neolithic pottery: distribution and sequence', *Proceedings of the Prehistoric Society*, Vol. 27, 174–233.

Case, H 1969 'Neolithic explanations', *Antiquity*, Vol. 43, 176–86.

Childs, J 2007 *The Williamite Wars in Ireland 1688–1691*. Hambledon Continuum, London.

Clancy, P 2006 'The Curragh Plains: a prehistoric landscape', *in* W Nolan & T McGrath (eds), *Kildare History and Society: interdisciplinary essays on the history of an Irish county*, 35–68. Geography Publications, Dublin.

Cleary, R M 1984 'Bone tempered Beaker potsherd', *Journal of Irish Archaeology*, Vol. 2, 73–5.

Cleary, R M 2000 'The potter's craft in prehistoric Ireland with specific reference to Lough Gur, Co. Limerick', *in* A Desmond, G Johnson, M McCarthy, J Sheehan & E Shee Twohig (eds), *New Agendas in Irish Prehistory: papers in commemoration of Liz Anderson*, 119–34. Wordwell, Bray.

Cleary, R M & Kelleher, H 2011 *Archaeological Excavations at Tullahedy, County Tipperary: Neolithic settlement in North Munster*. The Collins Press, Cork.

Coffey, G 1902 'A pair of brooches and chains of the Viking Period, recently found in Ireland', *Journal of the Royal Society of Antiquaries*, Vol. 32, 71.

Coles, J M 1973 *Archaeology by Experiment*. Hutchinson University Library, London.

Comber, M 2008 *The Economy of the Ringfort and Contemporary Settlement in Early Medieval Ireland*. British Archaeological Reports, International Series 1773. Archaeopress, Oxford.

Copley, M S, Berstan, R, Dudd, S N, Docherty, G, Mukherjee, A J, Straker, V, Payne, S & Evershed, R P 2003 'Direct chemical evidence for widespread dairying in prehistoric Britain', *Proceedings of the National Academy of Sciences of the USA*, Vol. 100, 1524–9.

Cross, T P & Slover, C H (eds) 1969 [originally published 1936] *Ancient Irish Tales*. Allen Figgis, Dublin.

Curle, A O 1923 *The Treasure of Traprain: a Scottish hoard of Roman silver plate*. Maclehose, Jackson & Co., Glasgow.

Danaher, E 2004 'Barnagore 4', *in* I Bennet (ed.), *Excavations 2002: summary accounts of archaeological excavations*, 61. Wordwell, Bray.

Danaher, E 2007 *Monumental Beginnings: the archaeology of the N4 Sligo Inner Relief Road*. NRA Scheme Monographs 1. National Roads Authority, Dublin.

David, N & Kramer, C 2001 *Ethnoarchaeology in Action*. Cambridge University Press, Cambridge.

Dehaene, G 2009 *Final Report on Site E3220 in Ballinapark Townland, Co. Wicklow*. Unpublished excavation report by Irish Archaeological Consultancy Ltd for Wicklow County Council and the National Roads Authority.

Delaney, F & Tierney, J 2011 *In the Lowlands of South Galway: archaeological excavations on the N18 Oranmore to Gort national road scheme*. NRA Scheme Monographs 7. National Roads Authority, Dublin.

Dillon, M (ed.) 1962 *Lebor na Cert. The Book of Rights*. Irish Texts Society, Dublin.

Doody, M 1988 'An Early Bronze Age Burial at Ballyveelish, Co. Tipperary', *Tipperary Historical Journal*, Vol. 18, 176–80.

Douglas, M 1966 *Purity and Danger: an analysis of the concepts of pollution and taboo* [2002 reprint]. Routledge, London.

Doyle, I W 1998 'The early medieval activity at Dalkey Island, Co. Dublin: a re-assessment', *Journal of Irish Archaeology*, Vol. 9, 89–103.

Doyle, I W 2009 'Mediterranean and Frankish pottery imports in Early Medieval Ireland', *Journal of Irish Archaeology*, Vol. 18, 17–62.

Doyle, M 2010 *Dress, personal ornament and bodily identities in early medieval Ireland: an archaeology of personhood*. Unpublished Ph.D thesis, University College Dublin.

Dunlop, C 2013 'Excavations of an early medieval rath and associated round houses at Crumlin recreation grounds', *Medieval Archaeology*, Vol. 57, 307–12.

Earwood, C 1993 *Domestic Wooden Artefacts in Britain and Ireland from Neolithic to Viking Times*. University of Exeter Press, Exeter.

Etchingham, C & Swift, C 2004 'English and Pictish Terms for Brooch in an 8th-century Irish Law-Text', *Medieval Archaeology*, Vol. 48, 31–49.

Evans, E E 1957 *Irish Folk Ways*. Routledge, London.

Evershed, R P 2008 'Experimental approaches to the interpretation of absorbed organic residues in archaeological ceramics', *World Archaeology*, Vol. 40, 26–47.

Fenton, A 1986 'Early yoke types in Britain', *in* A Fenton (ed.), *The Shape of the Past 2, Essays in Scottish Ethnology*, 35–46. John Donald, Edinburgh.

Ferguson, N 2006 *The Conservation and Management of the Battle of Aughrim as an Archaeological Landscape*. Unpublished MA Thesis, National University of Ireland, Galway.

FitzGerald, M 1997 'Insular Dress in Early Medieval Ireland', *Bulletin of the John Rylands University Library of Manchester*, Vol. 79, No. 3, 251–61.

Fitzpatrick, A (ed.) 2011 *The Amesbury Archer and the Boscombe Bowmen: bell beaker burials at Boscombe Down, Amesbury, Wiltshire*. Wessex Archaeology Ltd, Salisbury.

Flood, J & Flood, P 1999 *Kilcash 1190–1801*. Geography Publications, Dublin.

Flynn, C 2009 'Camlin 3: a cemetery-settlement in north Tipperary', *in* M Stanley, E Danaher & J Eogan (eds), *Dining and Dwelling*, 133–41. Archaeology and the National Roads Authority Monograph Series No. 6. National Roads Authority, Dublin.

Gosselain, O P 1992 'Technology and style: potters and pottery among Bafia of Cameroon', *Man*, Vol. 27, No. 3, 559–86.

Gosselain, O P 2000 'Materializing identities: an African perspective', *Journal of Archaeological Method and Theory*, Vol. 7, No. 3, 187–217.

Grogan, E & Kilfeather, A 1997 *Archaeological Inventory of County Wicklow*. The Stationery Office, Dublin.

Harbison, P 1986 'The Derrynaflan ladle: some parallels illustrated', *Journal of Irish Archaeology*, Vol. 3, 55–8.

Hencken, H O'N 1950 'Lagore crannog: an Irish royal residence of the 7th to 10th centuries AD', *Proceedings of the Royal Irish Academy*, Vol. 53C, 1–247.

Hill, P 1997 *Whithorn and St Ninian: the excavation of a monastic town 1984–91.* The Whithorn Trust, Sutton Publishing.

Hinds, K 2009 '193. Urchfont, Wiltshire: copper-alloy mount from a hanging bowl (PAS:WILT-1E76E1)', *in* M Lewis (ed.), *Portable Antiquities and Treasure Annual Report 2007*, 105. Department of Portable Antiquities and Treasure, British Museum, London.

Hirst, S M 1985 *An Anglo-Saxon Inhumation Cemetery at Sewerby, East Yorkshire.* York University Archaeological Publications 4. Department of Archaeology University of York, York.

Hodder, I 1982 *Symbols in Action: ethnoarchaeological studies of material culture.* Cambridge University Press, Cambridge.

Hodges, H 1989 *Artifacts: an introduction to early materials and technology.* Duckworth, London.

Hughes, J 2006 *Final Report on Archaeological Investigations at Sites 24–30 in the Townland of Granny, Co. Kilkenny, Vol. 1.* Unpublished report by Headland Archaeology Ltd for Waterford County Council and the National Roads Authority.

Hurcombe, L 2007 *Archaeological Artefacts as Material Culture.* Routledge, London & New York.

Jackman, N 2013 'Discovery and excavation', *in* N Jackman, C Moore & C Rynne, *The Mill at Kilbegly: an archaeological investigation on the route of the M6 Ballinasloe to Athlone national road scheme*, 11–44. NRA Scheme Monographs 12. National Roads Authority, Dublin.

Johnson, S A & Wailes, B 2007 *Dún Ailinne: excavations at an Irish Royal Site, 1968–1975.* University of Pennsylvania Museum of Archaeology and Anthropology, Philadelphia.

Jones, C 1998 'The Discovery and Dating of the Prehistoric Landscape of Roughan Hill in Co. Clare', *Journal of Irish Archaeology*, Vol. 9, 27–43.

Keily, J, Blackmore, L & Reilly, K 2012 'Antler and bone working', *in* R Cowie & L Blackmore, *Lundenwic: excavations in Middle Saxon London, 1987–2000*, 163–8. MOLA Monograph 63. Museum of London Archaeology, London.

Kelly, B, Roycroft, N & Stanley, M (eds) 2013 'Appendix 2—Dendrochronological dates from archaeological sites excavated on Irish national road schemes', *in* B Kelly, N Roycroft & M Stanley (eds), *Futures and Pasts: archaeological science on Irish road schemes*, 134–8. Archaeology and the National Roads Authority Monograph Series No. 10. National Roads Authority, Dublin.

Kelly, E P 2006 'Secrets of the bog bodies: the enigma of the Iron Age explained', *Archaeology Ireland*, Vol. 20, No. 1, 26–30.

Kelly, F 1988 *A Guide to Early Irish Law.* Early Irish Law Series Volume III. School of Celtic Studies, Dublin Institute for Advanced Studies, Dublin.

Kelly, F 1997 *Early Irish Farming: a study based mainly on the law-texts of the 7th and 8th centuries AD*. Dublin Institute for Advanced Studies, Dublin.

Kerr, T & McCormick, F 2014 'Statistics, sunspots and settlement: influences on sum of probability curves', *Journal of Archaeological Science*, Vol. 41, 493–501.

King, H A 1996 'New Graveyard, Clonmacnoise', *in* I Bennett (ed.), *Excavations 1995: summary accounts of archaeological excavations in Ireland*, 76–7. Wordwell, Bray.

King, H A 1998 'New Graveyard, Clonmacnoise', *in* I Bennett (ed.), *Excavations 1997: summary accounts of archaeological excavations in Ireland*, 149. Wordwell, Bray.

King, H A 2009 'The economy and industry of early medieval Clonmacnoise: a preliminary view', *in* N Edwards (ed.), *The Archaeology of the Early Medieval Celtic Churches*, 333–49. Society for Medieval Archaeology Monograph 29. Maney, Leeds.

Kinsella, T 1981 *An Duanaire 1600-1900: poems of the dispossessed*. The Dolmen Press, Portlaoise.

Koehler, C 2009 *Conservation Treatment Record, Reg. No. A022035:1:1, Lab. No. 2009:36*. Unpublished report by the National Museum of Ireland.

Lane, A & Campbell, E 2000 *Dunadd: an early Dalriadic capital*. Oxbow, Oxford.

Lanigan, H M 1964 *Jet bracelets in Ireland: rings of fossil wood*. Unpublished MA thesis, University College Dublin, Dublin.

Leach, E 1968 'Ritual', *in* D L Sills & R K Merton (eds), *International Encyclopedia of the Social Sciences*, 520–26. Macmillan and Free Press, New York.

Lemonnier, P 1993 'Introduction', *in* P Lemonnier (ed.), *Technological Choices: transformation in material cultures since the Neolithic*, 1–35. Routledge, London.

Linnane, S J & Kinsella, J 2009 *Report on the Archaeological Excavation of Baronstown 1, Co. Meath* (http://www.m3motorway.ie/Archaeology/Section2/Baronstown1/file,16723,en.pdf, accessed October 2013).

Lucy, S 1998 *The Early Anglo-Saxon Cemeteries of East Yorkshire. An analysis and reinterpretation*. BAR British Series 272. John & Erica Hedges, Oxford.

Lynn, C J & McDowell, J A 1988 'A note on the excavation of an early Christian period settlement in Deer Park Farms, Glenarm, 1984–1987', *The Glynns*, Vol. 16, 2–16.

Lynn, C J & McDowell, J A 2011 *Deer Park Farms: the excavation of a raised rath in the Glenarm Valley, Co. Antrim*. Northern Ireland Archaeological Monographs No. 9. The Stationery Office, Norwich.

MacNamidhe, M 1989 'The 'Buddha Bucket' from the Oseberg find', *Irish Arts Review*, Vol. 6, No. 3, 77–82.

MacNeill, E 1923 'Ancient Irish Law. The Law of Status or Franchise', *Proceedings of the Royal Irish Academy*, Vol. 36C, 265–316.

McCormick, F 2013 'Agriculture, settlement and society in Early Medieval Ireland', *Quaternary International*, Vol. 30, 1–12.

McDermott, C, Moore, C, Murray, C, Plunkett, G & Stanley, M 2009 'A Colossus of roads: the Iron Age archaeology of Ireland's peatlands', *in* G Cooney, K Becker, J Coles, M Ryan & S Sievers (eds), *Relics of Old Decency: archaeological studies in later prehistory. Festschrift for Professor Barry Raftery*, 49–64. Wordwell, Dublin.

Mandal, S, O'Sullivan, A, Byrnes, E, Weddle, D & Weddle, J 2004 'Archaeological experiments in the production of stone axeheads', *in* E Walker, F Wenban-Smith & F Healy (eds), *Lithics in Action*, 116–23. Oxbow Books, Oxford.

Mauss, M 1934 'Techniques of the body', *in* J Crary & S Kwinter (eds), *Incorporations* [1992 reprint], 455–77. Zone, New York.

Meaney, A L 1981 *Anglo-Saxon Amulets and Curing Stones*. BAR British Series 96. Oxford.

Medieval Pottery Research Group 1998 *A Guide to the Classification of Medieval Ceramic Forms*. Medieval Pottery Research Group Occasional Paper No. 1. Medieval Pottery Research Group Occasional, London.

Moore, C 2008 'Old routes to new research: the Edercloon wetland excavations in County Longford', *in* J O'Sullivan & M Stanley (eds), *Roads, Rediscovery and Research*, 1–12. Archaeology and the National Roads Authority Monograph Series No. 5. National Roads Authority, Dublin.

Moore, C 2009a *The Edercloon Artefact Assemblage: a study of the practice of object deposition at Edercloon, Co. Longford*. Unpublished Masters thesis, University College Dublin.

Moore, C 2009b *Report on worked wooden remains from Annaholty, Co. Tipperary E3530*. Unpublished report commissioned by TVAS (Ireland) Ltd.

Moore, C 2013 'Worked wood', *in* N Jackman, C Moore & C Rynne, *The Mill at Kilbegly: an archaeological investigation on the route of the M6 Ballinasloe to Athlone national road scheme*, 45–56. NRA Scheme Monographs 12. National Roads Authority, Dublin.

Moore, H 1986 *Space, Text and Gender*. Cambridge University Press, Cambridge.

Mount, C, Buckley, L & Lynch, P 1998 'Five Early Bronze Age cemeteries at Brownstown, Graney West, Oldtown and Ploopluck, County Kildare, and Strawhall, County Carlow', *Proceedings of the Royal Irish Academy*, Vol. 98C, No. 2, 25–99.

Needham, S 2004 'Migdale-Marnoch: sunburst of Scottish metallurgy', *in* I A G Shepard & G Barclay (eds), *Scotland in Ancient Europe: the Neolithic and Early Bronze Age of Scotland in their European Context*, 217–45. Society of Antiquaries of Scotland, Edinburgh.

Nelson, E C & Walsh, W F 1993 *Trees of Ireland native and naturalised*. The Lilliput Press, Dublin.

Newman, C 2002 'Ballinderry Crannóg No. 2, Co. Offaly: Pre-Crannóg Early Medieval Horizon', *Journal of Irish Archaeology*, Vol. 11, 99–123.

Ní Chonaill, B 2008 'Child-centred law in medieval Ireland', *in* R Davis & T Dunne (eds), *The Empty Throne: childhood and the crisis of modernity*, 1–31. Cambridge University Press, Cambridge.

O'Brien, E 1999 *Post-Roman Britain to Anglo-Saxon England: burial practices reviewed*. BAR British Series 289. Oxford.

O'Brien, E 2009 'Pagan or Christian? Burial in Ireland during the 5th to 8th Centuries AD', *in* N Edwards (ed.), *The Archaeology of the Early Medieval Celtic Churches. Proceedings of a Conference on the Archaeology of the Early Medieval Celtic Churches,*

September 2004, 135–54. The Society for Medieval Archaeology Monograph 29/ The Society for Church Archaeology Monograph 1. Maney, Leeds.

O Carroll, E 2013 'Wood selection and use', *in* N Jackman, C Moore & C Rynne, *The Mill at Kilbegly: archaeological investigation on the route of the M6 Ballinasloe to Athlone national road scheme*, 57–60. NRA Scheme Monographs 12. National Roads Authority, Dublin.

O'Connell, A 2009 'Excavations at Castlefarm—director's first findings', *in* M B Deevy & D Murphy (eds), *Places Along the Way: first findings on the M3*, 43–56. NRA Scheme Monographs 5. National Roads Authority, Dublin.

O'Connell, A & Clark, A 2009 *Report on the Archaeological Excavation of Castlefarm 1, Co. Meath* (http://www.m3motorway.ie/Archaeology/Section1/Castlefarm1/file,16711,en.pdf, accessed October 2013).

O'Curry, E 1873 *On the Manners and Customs of the Ancient Irish, Vol. 3*. W B Kelly, Dublin.

Ó Drisceoil, C 2001 'Site 2, Whiterath', *in* I Bennett (ed.), *Excavations 2000: summary accounts of archaeological excavations in Ireland*, 244. Wordwell, Bray.

Ó Floinn, R 1976 *Medieval cooking pottery in Leinster, thirteenth to fourteenth century*. Unpublished Masters thesis, University College Dublin.

Ó Floinn, R 1983 'The bronze strainer-ladle', *in* M Ryan (ed.), *The Derrynaflan Hoard 1: a preliminary account*, 31–4. National Museum of Ireland, Dublin.

Ó Floinn, R 1988 'Handmade medieval pottery in S.E. Ireland—"Leinster cooking ware"', *in* G Mac Niocaill & P F Wallace (eds), *Kemelia: studies in medieval archaeology and history in memory of Tom Delaney*, 325–48. Galway University Press, Galway.

Ó Floinn, R 1990 'Strainer-ladle', *in* S Youngs (ed.), '*The Work of Angels': masterpieces of Celtic metalwork, 6th–9th centuries AD*, 132. British Museum Publications, London.

Ó Floinn, R 2001 'Patrons and Politics: Art, Artefact and Methodology', *in* M Redknap, N Edwards, S Youngs, A Lane & J Knight (eds), *Pattern and Purpose in Insular Art: proceedings of the Fourth International Conference on Insular Art held at the National Museum & Gallery, Cardiff, 3–6 September 1998*, 1–14. Oxbow, Oxford.

Ó Floinn, R 2009 'The Anglo-Saxon Connection: Irish Metalwork, AD 400-800', *in* J Graham-Campbell & M Ryan (eds), *Anglo-Saxon/Irish Relations before the Vikings*, 231–51. Oxford University Press for the British Academy, Oxford.

O'Hanlon, J 1873 *Lives of the Irish Saints, Vol. 6*. James Duffy & Sons, Dublin.

O'Hara, R 2009a 'Early medieval settlement at Roestown 2', *in* M B Deevy & D Murphy (eds), *Places Along the Way: first findings on the M3*, 57–82. NRA Scheme Monographs 5. National Roads Authority, Dublin.

O'Hara, R 2009b 'Collierstown 1: a Late Iron Age–early medieval enclosed cemetery', *in* M B Deevy & D Murphy (eds), *Places Along the Way: first findings on the M3*, 83–100. NRA Scheme Monographs 5. National Roads Authority, Dublin.

O'Hara, R 2009c *Report on the Archaeological Excavation of Collierstown 1, Co Meath* (www.m3motorway.ie/Archaeology/Section2/Collierstown1/file,16721,en.pdf, accessed 29 March 2014).

Olsen, B 2013 *In Defense of Things: archaeology and the ontology of things*. Altamira Press, Lanha.

O'Mahony, T & Richey, A G (eds) 1873 *Senchus Mor (conclusion) being the Corus Bescna, or Customary Law and the Book of Aicill*. Ancient Laws of Ireland, vol. 3. Published under direction of the Commissioners for Publishing the Ancient Laws and Institutes of Ireland. Alexander Thom, Hodges Foster & Co., Dublin; Longmans, Green, Reader & Dyer, London.

O'Neill, T 2006 'Parknahown 5: an extensive cemetery at the River Goul', *Seanda*, No. 1, 32.

O'Neill, T 2007 'The hidden past of Parknahown, Co. Laois', *in* J O'Sullivan & M Stanley (eds), *New Routes to the Past*, 133–9. Archaeology and the National Roads Authority Monograph Series No. 4. National Roads Authority, Dublin.

O'Neill, T 2008 'Unearthing the past: discoveries at Parknahown, Co. Laois', *Ossory, Laois and Leinster*, Vol. 3, 1–24.

Ó Ríordáin, B & Waddell, J (eds) 1993 *The Funerary Bowls and Vases of the Irish Bronze Age*. Galway University Press, Galway.

O'Sullivan, A 2001 *Foragers, Farmers and Fishers in a Coastal Landscape: an intertidal archaeological survey of the Shannon estuary*. Discovery Programme Monographs No. 5. Royal Irish Academy, Dublin.

O'Sullivan, A & Nicholl, T 2011 'Early Medieval settlement enclosures in Ireland: dwellings, daily life and social identity', *Proceedings of the Royal Irish Academy*, Vol. 111C, 59–90.

O'Sullivan, A, McCormick, F, Harney, L & Kerr, T R 2014 *Early Medieval Ireland AD 400–100: the evidence from archaeological excavations*. Royal Irish Academy, Dublin.

O'Sullivan, J & Stanley, M (eds) 2006 'Appendix 1—Radiocarbon dates from excavated archaeological sites described in these proceedings', *in* J O'Sullivan & M Stanley (eds), *Settlement, Industry and Ritual*, 129–35. Archaeology and the National Roads Authority Monograph Series No. 3. National Roads Authority, Dublin.

O'Sullivan, J & Stanley, M (eds) 2008 'Appendix 1—Radiocarbon dates from excavated archaeological sites described in these proceedings', *in* J O'Sullivan & M Stanley (eds), *Roads, Rediscovery and Research*, 163–71. Archaeology and the National Roads Authority Monograph Series No. 5. National Roads Authority, Dublin.

Painter, K S 1977 *The Mildenhall Treasure: Roman silver from East Anglia*. British Museum Publications, London.

Painter, K S 1999 'The Water Newton Silver: votive or liturgical?', *Journal of the British Archaeological Association*, Vol. 152, 1–23.

Parker, R 1746 *Memoirs of the Most Remarkable Military Transactions from the Year 1683 to 1718*. Geo. and Alex. Ewing Booksellers, Dublin.

Raff, K 2011 *The Roman Banquet* (http://www.metmuseum.org/toah/hd/banq/hd_banq.htm, accessed October 2013).

Raftery, B 1995 'The conundrum of Irish Iron Age pottery', *in* B Raftery (ed.), *Sites and Sights of the Iron Age: essays on fieldwork and museum research presented to Ian Mathieson Stead*, 147–56. Oxbow Monograph 56. Oxbow, Oxford.

Raftery, J 1940 'Bronze Age Burials at Halverstown, Co. Kildare', *Journal of the Royal Society of Antiquaries of Ireland*, Vol. 10, No. 1, 57–61.

Raftery, J 1970 'Prehistoric coiled basketry bags', *Journal of the Royal Society of Antiquaries of Ireland*, Vol. 100, 167–8.

Reed, S, Bidwell, P & Allan, J 2011 'Excavation at Bantham, South Devon, and post-Roman trade in south-west England', *Medieval Archaeology*, Vol. 55, 82–138.

Reimer, P J, Baillie, M G L, Bard, E et al. 2004 'IntCal04 terrestrial radiocarbon age calibration, 0–26 cal kyr BP', *Radiocarbon*, Vol. 46, No. 3, 1029–58.

Riddler, I D & Trzaska–Nartowski, N I A 2012 '*Lundenwic* and the Middle Saxon Bone Interlude', *Anglo-Saxon Studies in Archaeology and History*, Vol. 18, 75–96.

Riddler, I & Trzaska–Nartowski, N I A (forthcoming) *Combs and Comb Making in Viking and Medieval Dublin*. Medieval Dublin Excavations 1962–81, Series B. National Museum of Ireland, Dublin.

Roche, H & Grogan, E 2006 'The N8 Rathcormac-Fermoy Bypass: the prehistoric pottery', in E Cotter, *N8 Rathcormac/Fermoy Bypass Scheme: Archaeological Services Contract, Phase 2 – Resolution*, 111–19. Unpublished report by Archaeological Consultancy Services Ltd.

Roux, V & Corbetta, D 1989 *The Potter's Wheel: craft specialization and technical competence*. Oxford and IBH Publishing, New Dehli.

Ryan, M 1987 'A suggested origin for the figure representations on the Derrynaflan paten', in E Rynne (ed.), *Figures from the Past: studies on figurative art in Christian Ireland in honour of Helen M Roe*, 62–72. Glendale Press, Dún Laoghaire, for the Royal Society of Antiquaries of Ireland.

Sabin, D & Donaldson, K 2005 *Archaeological Surveys Metal Detection Report: N6 Galway to Ballinasloe National Road Scheme Luttrell's Pass A024/5.1*. Unpublished report for ArchaeoPhysica Ltd on behalf of Galway County Council.

Salque, M 2012 'Was milk processed in these ceramic pots? Organic residue analyses of European prehistoric cooking vessels', in F Feulner, N L Doorn & M Leonardi (eds), *May Contain Traces of Milk: investigating the role of dairy farming and milk consumption in the European Neolithic*, 129–41. University of York, York.

Schulting, R, Sheridan, A, Crozier, R & Murphy, E 2010 'Revisiting Quanterness: new AMS dates and stable isotope data from an Orcadian chamber tomb', *Proceedings of the Society of Antiquaries of Scotland*, Vol. 140, 1–50.

Seager Smith, R 2000 'Worked Bone and Antler', in A J Lawson (ed.), *Potterne 1982–5: animal husbandry in later prehistoric Wiltshire*, 222–40. Wessex Archaeology Report 17. Wessex Archaeology, Salisbury.

Seaver, M 2006 'Through the mill—excavation of an early medieval settlement at Raystown, County Meath', in J O'Sullivan & M Stanley (eds), *Settlement, Industry and Ritual*, 73–87. Archaeology and the National Roads Authority Monograph Series No. 3. National Roads Authority, Dublin.

Seaver, M 2009 *Report on Archaeological Excavation of Site 21, Raystown, Co. Meath*. Unpublished report by CRDS Ltd for Meath County Council.

Seaver, M 2010 'Against the grain: early medieval settlement and burial on the

Blackhill. Excavations at Raystown, Co. Meath', *in* C Corlett & M Potterton (eds), *Death and burial in early medieval Ireland*, 261–80. Wordwell, Dublin.

Seaver, M 2012 'Early Medieval Bone- and Antler-Working', *in* T Kerr, M Doyle, M Seaver, F McCormick & A O'Sullivan, *Industrial Activity on Rural Secular Sites in Ireland, A.D. 400-1100*, 59–65. EMAP Report 6.1 (http://www.emap.ie/documents/EMAP2012_EarlyMed_Industry_on_Rural_Sites.pdf, accessed October 2013).

Sheehan, J 1998 'Early Viking Age silver hoards from Ireland', *in* H B Clarke, M Ní Mhaonaigh & R Ó Floinn (eds), *Ireland and Scandinavia in the Early Viking Age*, 166–202. Four Courts Press, Dublin.

Sheehan, J 2009 'The peacock's tale: excavations at Caherlehillan, Iveragh, Ireland', *in* N Edwards (ed.), *The Archaeology of the Early Medieval Celtic Churches*, 191–206. Society for Medieval Archaeology Monograph 29/Society for Church Archaeology Monograph 1. Maney Publishing, Leeds.

Sheridan, A 1993 'The manufacture, production and use of Irish bowls and vases', *in* B Ó Ríordáin & J Waddell (eds), *The Funerary Bowls and Vases of the Irish Bronze Age*, 45–75. Galway University Press, Galway.

Sheridan, A 1995 'Irish Neolithic pottery: the story in 1995', *in* I A Kinnes & G Varndell (eds), *'Unbaked urns of rudely shape': essays on British and Irish pottery for Ian Longworth*, 3–21. Oxbow, Oxford.

Sheridan, A 2007 'From Picardie to Pickering and Pencraig Hill? New information on the 'Carinated Bowl Neolithic' in northern Britain', *in* A Whittle & V Cummings (eds), *Going Over: the Mesolithic-Neolithic transition in north-west Europe*, 441–92. Oxford University Press for The British Academy, Oxford.

Sheridan, A & Bayliss, A 2008 'Pots and time in Bronze Age Ireland', *Antiquity*, Vol. 82, 204–7.

Sherratt, A 1981 'Plough and pastoralism: aspects of the secondary products revolution', *in* I Hodder, G Isaac & N Hammond (eds), *Pattern of the Past: studies in honour of David Clarke*, 261–305. Cambridge University Press, Cambridge.

Simms, J G 1977 'The Battle of Aughrim: history and poetry', *Irish University Review*, Vol. 7, No. 1, 36–51.

Simms, K 1987 *From Kings to Warlords: the changing political structure of Gaelic Ireland in the later middle ages*. Boydell Press, Suffolk.

Smyth, J 2014 *Settlement in the Irish Neolithic: new discoveries at the edge of Europe*. Prehistoric Society/Oxbow, Oxford.

Stanley, M, Danaher, E & Eogan, J (eds) 2010 'Appendix 1—Radiocarbon dates from excavated archaeological sites described in these proceedings', *in* M Stanley, E Danaher & J Eogan (eds), *Creative Minds: production, manufacturing and invention in ancient Ireland*, 117–27. Archaeology and the National Roads Authority Monograph Series No. 7. National Roads Authority, Dublin.

Story, G 1693 *A Continuation of the Impartial History of the Wars in Ireland from the Time That Duke Schonberg Landed with an Army in that Kingdom, to the 23rd march 1691/2 when their Majesties Proclamation was Published, Declaring the War to be Ended*. Ric. Chiswell, London.

Stuijts, I 2005 'Wood and charcoal identification', *in* M Gowen, J Ó Néill & M Phillips (eds), *The Lisheen Mine Archaeological Project 1996–8*, 139–84. Wordwell, Bray.

Talma, A S & Vogel, J C 1993 'A simplified approach to calibrating ^{14}C dates', *Radiocarbon*, Vol. 35, No. 2, 317–32.

Taylor, K 2007 'Prehistoric features and an early medieval enclosure at Coonagh West, Co. Limerick', *in* J O'Sullivan & M Stanley (eds), *New Routes to the Past*, 73–9. Archaeology and the National Roads Authority Monograph Series No. 4. National Roads Authority, Dublin.

Taylor, K 2008 'At home and on the road: two Iron Age sites in Co. Tipperary', *Seanda*, No. 3, 54–5.

Taylor, K 2010 'Masters of their craft: worked wood from Annaholty, Co. Tipperary', *Seanda*, No. 5, 8–9.

Taylor, M 1981 *Wood in Archaeology*. Shire Publications, Aylesbury.

Thomas, C 1988 'The context of Tintagel: a new model for the diffusion of post-Roman Mediterranean imports', *Cornish Archaeology*, Vol. 27, 7–25.

Thomas, C 1990 'Gallici nautae de Galliarum provinciis' – a sixth/seventh century trade with Gaul, reconsidered', *Medieval Archaeology*, Vol. 34, 1–26.

Tierney, J 1998 'Wood and woodlands in Early Medieval Munster', *in* M A Monk & J Sheehan (eds), *Early Medieval Munster: archaeology, history and Society*, 53–8. Cork University Press, Cork.

Ulbricht, I 1978 *Die Geweihverarbeitung in Haithabu*, Die Ausgrabungen in Haithabu 7. Karl Wachholtz Verlag, Neumünster.

Waddell, J 2010 *The Prehistoric Archaeology of Ireland* (2nd edn). Wordwell, Bray.

Wallace, A 2010 'Excavation of an early medieval cemetery at Ratoath, Co. Meath', *in* C Corlett & M Potterton (eds), *Death and Burial in Early Medieval Ireland in the light of recent archaeological excavations*, 295–316. Wordwell, Dublin.

Wallace, P W & Ó Floinn, R (eds) 2002 *Treasures of the National Museum of Ireland: Irish antiquities*. Gill & Macmillan, Dublin.

Walsh, F 2006 'Neolithic Monanny, Co. Monaghan', *in* J O'Sullivan & M Stanley (eds), *Settlement, Industry and Ritual*, 7–17. Archaeology and the National Roads Authority Monograph Series No. 3. National Roads Authority, Dublin.

Walsh, F 2009 *Site 110: Monanny 1*. Unpublished report by Irish Archaeological Consultancy Ltd for Monaghan County Council and the National Roads Authority.

Walsh, F, Lyons, S & McClatchie, M 2011 'A post-built Early Neolithic house at Kilmainham, Co. Meath', *Archaeology Ireland*, Vol. 25, No. 3, 35–7.

Walton Rogers, P 2005 'Dyestuff analysis on E ware pottery', *in* A Crone & E Campbell, *A Crannog of the First Millennium AD: excavations by Jack Scott at Loch Glashan, Argyll, 1960*, 61–2. The Society of Antiquaries of Scotland, Edinburgh.

Walton Rogers, P 2007 *Cloth and Clothing in Early Anglo-Saxon England, AD 450–700*. CBA Research Report 145. Council for British Archaeology, York.

Warner, R B 1979 'The Clogher yellow layer', *Medieval Ceramics*, Vol. 3, 37–40.

Warner, R B 1985–6 'The date of the start of Lagore', *Journal of Irish Archaeology*, Vol. 3, 75–7.

Wason, P K 2004 *The Archaeology of Rank*. Cambridge University Press, Cambridge.

Westphalen, P 1999 'Die Kleinfunde aus der frühgeschichtlichen Wurt Elisenhof', *Offa-Bücher*, Vol. 80, 1–232.

White Marshall, J & Walsh, C 2005 *Illaunloughan Island: an early medieval monastery in County Kerry*. Wordwell, Bray.

Whitfield, N 2006 'Dress and Accessories in the Early Irish Tale "The Wooing of Becfhola"', *Medieval Clothing and Textiles*, Vol. 2, 1–34.

Whittle, A, Healy, F & Bayliss, A 2011 *Gathering Time: dating the Early Neolithic enclosures of southern Britain and Ireland*. Oxbow, Oxford.

Wiggins, K 2006a 2006:1172. Killeany, Co. Laois (http://www.excavations.ie, accessed October 2013).

Wiggins, K 2006b 'A tale of two cemeteries', *Seanda*, No. 1, 33–5.

Wiggins, K 2009 *Report on the archaeological excavations of Killeany 1, Co. Laois, Ministerial Directions A015/061, E2171*. Unpublished report by Archaeological Consultancy Services Ltd for Laois County Council.

Wilde, W R 1863 *A Descriptive Catalogue of the Antiquities in the Museum of the Royal Irish Academy. Vol. 1. Articles of Stone, Earthen, Vegetable, and Animal Materials; and of Copper and Bronze*. Hodges Smith & Co., Dublin.

Wood, J 2001 *Prehistoric Cooking*. Tempus, Stroud.

Wood, J 2009 *Tasting the Past: recipes from the Stone Age to the Present*. The History Press, Stroud.

Wooding, J M 1996 *Communication and Commerce Along the Western Sealanes AD 400–800*. British Archaeological Reports, International Series 654. Oxford.

Woolgar, C M 2006 *The Senses in Late Medieval England*. Yale University Press, New Haven & London.

Youngs, S (ed.) 1989 *'The Work of Angels': masterpieces of Celtic metalwork, 6th–9th centuries A.D.* British Museum Publications, London.

Youngs, S & Herepath, N 2001 'Cumbria: Arnside', *in* H Geake (ed.), 'Medieval Britain and Ireland 2000: Portable Antiquities Scheme', *Medieval Archaeology*, Vol. 45, 237–8.